THE TEARS OF JESUS
The Central Passion of the Gospel

L. R. SCARBOROUGH, B.A., D.D.

D1096387

THE TEARS OF JESUS

Sermons to Aid Soul-Winners

BY

L. R. SCARBOROUGH, B.A., D.D.

PRESIDENT AND PROFESSOR OF EVANGELISM IN THE SOUTHWESTERN
BAPTIST THEOLOGICAL SEMINARY

BAKER BOOK HOUSE
Grand Rapids, Michigan

Reprinted 1967 by
Baker Book House Company

Reprinted from the original
edition published in 1922

PHOTOLITHOPRINTED BY CUSHING - MALLOY, INC.
ANN ARBOR, MICHIGAN, UNITED STATES OF AMERICA
1967

FOREWORD

I have preached all of the sermons in this volume in some four or five hundred evangelistic meetings throughout the Southern States in the last twenty-five years, in which meetings there have been many, many thousands of people saved. They are taken down by my secretary just as I preached them in July, 1921, in a great tabernacle meeting in Duncan, Oklahoma; and without much careful revision are sent out with the prayer and the hope that they will help many workers for Jesus Christ to be better winners of souls and to aid in the creation of an evangelistic atmosphere in which it will be easy for men to find Jesus Christ. No great period of soul-winning can come about except in an evangelistic atmosphere charged and surcharged with the Gospel of Jesus Christ and the power of His Spirit.

These sermons preached to many, many thousands, through the mercy of God, have created an evangelistic atmosphere, caused many thousands of Christians to have the central passion of the Gospel, a burden for lost souls and a spiritual yearning to lead them to know the Savior. And it is in the fond hope that a wider circulation of the truth here presented will bear fruit in creating

a passion for souls and an atmosphere in which
they can be saved, that this volume of sermons is
sent out affectionately and in the hope of a fade-
less immortality. May a contemplation of the
compassion of Jesus Christ for a lost world cause
God's people everywhere to have the hunger He
had when He lived and died and rose again, and in
endless intercession for us seeks the world's redemption.

L. R. S.

CONTENTS

THE TEARS OF JESUS

THE TEARS OF JESUS

CHAPTER I

THE TEARS OF JESUS

John 11:35—Jesus Weeping at the Gate of Death.
Lu. 19:41—Jesus Weeping over a Doomed City.
Heb. 5:7—Jesus Weeping over a Lost World.

I read three passages of scripture:

John 11:35—"Jesus Wept."

Luke 19:41—"And when he was come near, he beheld the city, and wept over it."

Heb. 5:7—"Who in the days of his flesh, when he had offered up prayers and supplications with strong crying and tears unto him that was able to save him from death, and was heard in that he feared."

We find in this first scripture Jesus weeping at the grave of Lazarus. In this second scripture we find Him weeping over a city which being doomed had rejected His message. And in the last scripture we find Him shedding tears and offering prayers in the days of His flesh over a ruined world for which He was to die.

We find in this second scripture that He was coming to Jerusalem for the last time. He had been out among the people for three and a half

years, preaching, teaching, healing and perform-
ing many miracles. The blind could see when he
touched their eyes; the lame could walk, the dumb
could speak, and the dead came forth out of the
grave at His word of authority and power. But
He had come now to Jerusalem for the last time.
Just a few days afterwards he was crucified in
the city he had come to save; and coming in that
morning from the east side, with a great crowd
meeting Him and following Him, praising God in
accordance with the promises concerning Him, as
He came up over the crest of Mount Olivet He saw
that beautiful city with a wonderful history. I
am sure, since He knew all things, there was present in His mind the past history of triumphs, of
defeat, of prosperity and adversity. I am sure
that He saw with His historic mind the things
that had transpired in that city—there where a
great people had builded a great city, the center
of the religious life of the world, where He had
trained a race to be His chosen people. And as
He looked upon that city the scriptures say ''He
wept.'' This Son of God, this Son of Man, seeing
that city wept bitter, briny tears over what He
saw. This is one of the three times in the scriptures where it speaks of the tears of Jesus. On
one occasion before this He stood at the grave of
one of His friends, the grave of Lazarus, and
wept, joined in the sorrow of the loved ones for
the man who had been hospitable to Him, a man
He loved. And there the Son of Man at the gate

of death shed tears. And the other time where
it speaks of His tears is where I read you from
the 5th chapter of Hebrews. It says that "in the
days of His flesh with strong supplication and
tears he prayed unto Him Who was able to save
Him from death." There in that case Jesus Christ
not only wept over a lost city, but He wept over a
lost world.

Now I want us to think for a little while of the
weeping Savior—the tears of Jesus Christ.

WHOSE ARE THESE TEARS?

Who is this strange person who has filled all
history and yet who standing on the crest of the
mountain we see weeping? His heart is torn and
there comes from His eyes and from His heart
tears that represent the attitude of His soul toward a lost city and toward the lost world. Who
is He? Why He is the author of our Bible, the
founder of our churches, a refuge to our souls, the
hope of our resurrection, the builder of our
heaven, and the source, the provider of all our
spiritual blessings. The scriptures call Him
our advocate, the alpha and omega of our spiritual life, the ancient of days, the anointed one, the
balm in Gilead for our souls, the bread of life
for our strength, the day-spring and morning
star of our hopes, the corner stone and the foundation of our lives, the commander of God's army
which is to conquer all sin, the counsellor and wis-
dom and guide for our feet. He is the founder

and the fountain on which we build and from which we drink. He is the hiding place for our tempest-tossed souls, the high priest of our communion with God; He is the Immanuel, the very presence of the Most High. He is King over Kings and Lord over Lords. He was the Lamb of God slain from before the foundation of the world as a sacrifice and atonement for our sins. He is the leader of God's mightiest hosts, the Lion of the Tribe of Judah. He it was that was the Man of Sorrows and who was acquainted with grief. He is the conquerer over sin and the enemies of God, the mediator between man and God, the messenger of God's covenant to a lost world, the Messiah of hope for a coming day of full redemption. He is the Prince of Life and the Prince of Peace, the redeemer, the rock of ages, the rose of Sharon, the scepter of Israel, the shepherd of God's sheep. He is God's only begotten and most beloved son; and here on the mount overlooking Jerusalem He weeps with a heart full of compassion and love for a lost world and establishes here again the doctrine of the chief and central and supreme passion of the gospel wrought out in His ministry and death and intercession for a sin-cursed world. He is the mightiest among the mighty and loveliest among ten thousand, the maker and preserver of our lives and the Savior of our souls; He it is that weeps over our sin and doom and destiny. It is in His hands that the reins of the universe are

held. This man is the Son of God, is very God
Himself. He it is who controls all the things of
our lives; and yet yonder in the city where He had
taught and preached and was soon to be crucified,
we see Him shedding the bitterest of tears. He is
not some conqueror come to destroy, but a Savior
come to save. He will not call down the wrath of
the clouds and gather the powers of the storms
to destroy those people. He has come to weep
over them and die for them and save them. He
it is that is weeping today over a lost world.

I raise another question.

WHY THESE TEARS?

Why is it that this Son of Man, this Son of
God, is weeping over the city of Jerusalem, and
was constantly during the days of His flesh ap-
pealing unto God with strong supplications and
tears? I say to you He is not weeping for Himself, though He sees the shadow of the cross
just ahead of Him, He sees the dark, unspeakable sorrow of Gethsemane through which He is
to go, the cruel crown of thorns which is to be
pressed on His head, and though already doubtless the pierce of the nails is in His hand and the
sword in His side. Yet He is not weeping over
Himself. He is not weeping like a defeated conqueror. He was not weeping over a life of defeat, though in the eyes of the world He was living a life of defeat. He was not weeping because
of His own failure or because of any discontent

in His heart. Jesus was not weeping for Himself; but He was weeping because He saw some things from the Mount of Olivet. He was not weeping over that city which through the centuries had been builded by the sacrifices and labors of His people. He was not weeping for its reputation, though He saw the ruin of that city about which He here prophesied. He was not weeping for the falling walls and the ruins of the Temple. Why was He weeping that day? What was it that He saw that caused the tears to come from His eyes? It is about that that I wish to speak to you.

I want if I can to bring you this day into a sympathetic attitude with Jesus Christ, as He stood on Mount Olivet. What was it that brought the tears from His eyes and broke His heart? It lies in three directions. In the first place, he wept because He saw the spiritual *condition* of men; He saw men in their sins; He saw them in the darkness of their unbelief, in the night of their unfaith in Him, sinners, dead in trespasses and sins; He saw the wrath of God on them if the love of God was not in their hearts; He saw them rejecting the only light come to them. He saw them without hope and without God in the world. As He looked upon the soul of an unbeliever no wonder it brought tears to His eyes, no wonder it brought a desire to be crucified for the life and salvation of that individual. The condition of

men today ought to bring tears and burdens to
the hearts of God's people.

I stood the other day by the side of a wife as
she looked upon the pale, emaciated face of her
loving and affectionate husband. The doctors
had just operated on him and said he had typhoid fever. At that time he was suffering from
a hemorrhage which it looked like he could not
stand. His face was white and his finger tips and
toe tips seemed to be drained of blood. I stood
by her side as we went into another room to pray.
Oh, there was such a wringing of the wife's heart
as she said, "He cannot stand the loss of blood!
He cannot stand the battle of the germs of disease in his body!" She realized the condition of
her husband.

I stood by the side of a mother as she looked
into the face of, as she thought, her dying baby.
Her heart was wrung. The doctors had said,
"He must die." She was torn by the realization
of the condition of her child.

I will tell you, my friends, we need today to
look into the lives of the unsaved men all about
us and see their peril and condition before Almighty God. Every man and woman and young
person in this community without Jesus Christ in
their hearts by faith, is lost and dead in trespasses and in sins, is away from God and has no
hope. The immoral decay of sin is in every particle of their spirit. Shall we look on them un-
moved while the Son of God seeing a lost and

ruined city shed tears over its condition? I trust
that God's people seeing the unsaved about them
today and during this meeting will join the Savior
in weeping over a lost world.

I shall never forget when my first child, just
five years of age, a little boy (one Sunday afternoon, after I had preached in the morning), as
I was lying on my bed was sitting astride my
body. Suddenly he changed the subject from
what we had been talking about and looking into
my face he said with a trembling voice, "Daddy,
I am lost. I want you to show me the way to
Christ." I do not explain it. I only tell you the
story. It was the first time I realized the spiritual condition of my child. It was the first time
he had appealed to me from his own lost soul.
From that time until he was saved I kept the
prayers hot up to God. I carried him to the Savior day by day. I believe it was because of the
concern created in my heart that day that I kept
the prayers hot. I want us in these days to remember the spiritual condition of every man that
does not know Jesus Christ.

I think another thing that stirred the heart of
Jesus was not only the condition of men, but the
destiny of men He saw, the place to which these
people were going when they were carried to the
cemeteries. He was thinking of their destiny.
He was thinking of their destiny, not their power.
He the Son of God was thinking of where those
people were going after death. And it is a mat-

ter that should stir our hearts—not what we possess here. Not a question of how much education or how little we have, but the question of destiny, of where you are going, should be the important question. It matters not that we die. How little value there is to the bodies of men, how little value! But my friends it is the eternal destiny of the soul that is the important question. I want us to know in the battle that we are going to fight here within the next few days that we are fighting a battle for the destinies of men. Every unsaved man in your community is going to hell. I do not know how you feel over here. I bless God I know there is a heaven for those who believe in Christ and a hell for those who do not believe in Christ. I am going to preach the gospel on this point. I want us to see the destinies of men and be moved like our Savior was moved.

There was another thing that stirred the heart of our Savior and that was *their refusal to hear Him and their rejection of Him.* Oh, the saddest thing that can come to the heart of Jesus Christ is for Him to be rejected! I wonder what will be the attitude of the people of this community. Jesus there looked upon that sinning, wicked city. He had wrought among them and yet they had rejected Him. I tell you, there is a demonstration on every hand that Jesus Christ is the Son of God and the Savior of the world. I wonder what we will do with this demonstration the next few days.

This incident in the life of the Savior but illustrates the care Jesus has for men.

THE SAVIOR'S CARE

He has shown, not only in His earthly life and sacrificial death, but in His heavenly ministry for these twenty centuries how much He cares for men. Even the hairs of our heads are numbered and not a sparrow falls without His loving care. Every detail of our lives is of interest to the Savior and all those things that make for our salvation and spiritual strength and service for Him are of the deepest concern to our Savior's heart. Does He not show in His attitude at Lazarus' grave that He loves and cares for the suffering loved ones at every grave? Does He not show by the many examples of healing, of raising the dead, of straightening the limbs of the crippled, opening the eyes of the blind and the ears of the deaf, that He cares for our bodies and our souls? Never a tear falls from the heart of a sorrowing widow nor from the penitent soul of the sick sinner that misses the loving care of our Savior. He has shown it in giving us the Bible with its many promises. He has assured us of it by His multiplied providences of loving care. That is the beauty of that great picture on Mount Olivet. Jesus loves men and has a concern for their salvation. He has shown it in His creative power, in His preserving, providential power, in

His earthly ministry and in His death on Calvary.

You and I should take up the work of Jesus Christ and care for lost men. This is the message that I bring you this morning. This is the message— do you care for the lost men and women of this city? I wonder how many of you do. Will you stand with Jesus on Mount Olivet today and say, "We, too, will weep for our loved ones and join our Savior in caring for their souls?"

Some time ago I was in a great convention. I spoke to that convention on compassion for the lost. It was some years ago when our boys were gathering in the army camps all over our country. In that crowd was a rather old, plainly dressed woman. She and her husband were messengers to that convention evidently from some inland church. When the service was over she and her husband came down the aisle to shake hands with me. She took me by the hand and said, "Do you live at Fort Worth?" I said, "I do." Then she started to say, "My boy is in Camp Bowie near Fort Worth." She stopped and wept. Seeing her weeping her husband came up and putting his arm around her, he said, "Mary, what's the matter?" She said, "I was thinking of our baby boy yonder in Camp Bowie. You know he isn't saved. We have written letters to him about it; we have prayed for him and others have prayed for him." She said, "Here's a preacher that lives near where our soldier boy is and I was trying to put our boy, our baby boy, on the heart of this preacher." Then she turned to me in a way and with a question I shall never forget. I thought I loved lost men. For twenty-five years I have given strength without reservation to the winning of lost men to Christ. I thought I loved lost men. But this dear old mother looked up with all the love of a mother and said *"Preacher, do you love lost men?"* Oh, that question rings in my heart today!

You have made great preparation for this meeting and I bless God for it. The great question now is, Do we love lost men? If we do, God help us to join Jesus Christ in soul-agony for them that we may win them to Him. I wonder how many of you can say, "Deep down in my heart I do have a tender affectionate concern for the unsaved of this community and I can join with my Savior in a deep compassion for their salvation."

Listen to what God says, "They that sow in tears shall reap in joy. He that goeth forth and weepeth, bearing precious seed, shall doubtless come again with rejoicing, bringing his sheaves with him." God help us to be stirred in our souls for the lost of this community.

CHAPTER II

THE ESSENTIALS OF AN EVANGELISTIC VICTORY

Isa. 38:1-6.

I am going to read you about a sick king.

"In those days was Hezekiah sick unto death. And Isaiah the prophet the son of Amoz came unto him, and said unto him, Thus saith the Lord":

My friends, it is a very important time for your soul when God speaks to you whether you are sick or well. Now listen to what God said to this very sick man:

"Set thine house in order; for thou shalt die, and not live. Then Hezekiah turned his face toward the wall, and prayed unto the Lord." Men usually pray when they get sick. They turn to God in the time when their lives are imperiled. This good king when he received God's message turned to God in prayer and said: (I call your attention to this prayer. It is a very short prayer. I call your attention to what he did not pray for. I do not know what I would ask God for if I were on my dying pillow. I do not think I would pray the prayer that Hezekiah prayed. I am quite sure I could not pray that prayer. It is a wonderful prayer in what he did not ask and in what he did ask. Notice what he said.)

"Remember now, O Lord, I beseech thee, how I have walked" not before my neighbor, not before my family, not before my closest friends, but "how I have walked before thee" before the all-seeing eye of God who knows our thoughts, reads aright our lives.

"Remember now, O Lord, I beseech thee, how I have walked before thee in truth and with a perfect heart."

That was his inside religion—how God saw him as he was on the inside. You can deceive your closest friends for a while, even the most intimate members of your family you can deceive for a while; but you cannot deceive God. He knows you as you are. He sees you as your soul is; and when you call on God to see how you walk before Him you may know that the record He makes is true and what He sees are the facts in your life.

And then he said:

"Remember I have done that which was good in thy sight." That was his outside life before men, how he walked before men, how he lived before them.

"And Hezekiah wept sore."

Some great men weep. I read the story of how Carpentier's manager stood over the crumpled form of the man whose destiny he promoted and wept. They told me that in the most tragical time of the recent war, when it looked like defeat was coming to the forces of freedom, when the cloud of unspeakable darkness of German dominance seemed to weep over all Europe and threatened to spread over this country, that the Secretary of our great war President, Woodrow Wilson, came into Mr. Wilson's private office one morning and found him weeping, with his heart breaking. The secretary said to him, "Mr. President, why these tears?" He said, "I am weeping for the imperiled liberties of the world."

Here is a great man, a good king of Judah weeping because of broken health and because of a disordered kingdom. He needed to set his house in order; and on what he thought his dying pillow, he had wept sore. It seemed that Isaiah had withdrawn for the moment from the weeping king and later God sent the prophet back to him. And God said unto Isaiah:

"Go, and say to Hezekiah, Thus saith the Lord, the God of David thy father, I have heard thy prayer."

The first message was the message to the disordered house and dying body. The second message, after he had cried and prayed was:

"I have heard thy prayer."

Oh, what a good message! I wonder how many of you Christian people have gotten the answer to your prayer—as you prayed, God's wireless

brought back to you an answer from God. I have
had those experiences, when God has said, when
the prayer was ended, "I have heard thy prayer.
I have sent forth the answer." I wonder how
many of you have gotten the answer to your
prayers for a great revival in your city. I wonder how many of you have "prayed through" this
meeting. You have advertised it remarkably
well. I have been in a great many oil towns. I
have been in a great many places where the com-
mercial and industrial interests of the people
were predominant. But I want to say that I have
never been in a town where there seemed to be
such a great spirit of liberality and Christianity
as is manifested on the pages of the daily papers
in your city in advertising this meeting. You
have made plans; you have invested a consider-
able amount of money; you have heralded this
meeting and organized for it far and wide; and
I bless God for the preparation and publicity
you have made. But I ask you a very much more
important question. How many of you have
prayed through and gotten your answer from God
that He will give in answer to prayer and re-
sponses to the gospel a great soul-sweeping, com-
munity-wide revival? "Go tell the dying king
that I have heard his prayer."

And the second part of the message was "I
have seen thy tears." Oh, what a glorious word
from heaven that God as He sits regnant on His

throne sees the tears of the child of God as they come from a broken heart. Why this same God was able to make a world, or a thousand or a billion worlds, and yet He said, "I saw the tears trickling down the cheek of one of my servants." I bless God that there is no tear of the broken-hearted widow, there is no tear of the penitent sinner in all the wide world that misses the attention of Almighty God.

"I have seen thy tears." "I have heard thy prayer."

Notice another thing he says:

"Behold I will add unto thy days fifteen years." Remember that God said to him in the first message, "Thou shalt die, and not live." And here the cry of faith seems to have reversed the judgment of God. Prayer and tears made the king over and gave him a new lease on life. That was a personal blessing. I wonder tonight how many people there are here who need a personal blessing. Some of you have lost your grip on God through gold or the desire for it, or in laboring to make bread for your family, or pleasure or something else has come into your life and has released your grip on God. Once you prayed; now you do not. Once you loved the Bible; now you do not. Once you were an attendant upon the worship of God; now you are not. Once you lived a consistent, prayerful life; but now your life is covered with sin. I wonder how many of you tonight can pray that God will give you a new lease on your spiritual life, that you may come back to Him and be worth while in His Kingdom.

"I will give you fifteen years."

I will give you a personal blessing.
But that is not all he says:

"Tell him that I will not only give him fifteen years, a personal blessing, but tell him I will deliver thee and this city out of the hand of the king of Assyria: and I will defend this city." There was a community blessing. Oh, my friends tonight I wonder how many of you have been engulfed and conquered and mastered by the desire to get rich in a little while from these oil fields that are about you and I wonder how many of you have lost your faith and grip on God because of this greed for gold. Oh, the engulfing power of materialism. I wonder how many of you would like to see your city delivered from the power of sin that your people may come back to God. God says, "I have heard thy prayers and seen thy tears. I will give you a personal blessing and a community blessing. Not only that, but I will defend your city." God says I will give you a permanent blessing, a blessing that will not pass with the passing of your prosperity and with the passing seasons. But I will establish here my throne. I will build up your city walls and I will become a defender of your city.

Now, on the basis of this wondrous story in the

Old Testament I want to take it out of its life back yonder twenty-five or twenty-eight hundred years ago and bring it and apply it to your city and to your need. I see in this incident the three great essentials for a revival of religion. I will tell you, my friends, that great revivals of religion come down from God and they are based on human conditions. I know that God wants to give to this city a great revival. It is promised in the Bible; it is the very word of the Divine Spirit and I know the Divine Heart is yearning and that Divine power is ready. But, as Jesus Christ, the mighty Son of God, could not perform many miracles in the place where He was reared, Nazareth, because of their unbelief, so tonight, my friends, God cannot and will not impose a revival on a people who are unwilling to pay the price of it. These three conditions are as follows:

First there must be

PRAYER

God's people must pray for the power of God, pray for the preacher and the preachers, pray for the singers, pray for each other, pray for the Christian people, pray for themselves, and pray for our unsaved, lost friends. Twenty-five years of almost incessant labor in trying to win men to Christ has convinced me by a thousand arguments that it is the prayer of God's people that brings down the power of God and creates the evangelistic atmosphere. All of God's people can work at this task. You will not leave it to the pastor, or to this preacher, or to the officers of the church. Thank God, the simplest man, the youngest child, the oldest man or woman, can work at this great job of getting the power of God down on this community. Prayer is an absolute essential. And if you have made up your mind to be prayerless, God will make this a powerless community.

"If ye being evil know how to give good gifts unto your children, how much more shall your heavenly Father give the Holy Spirit to them that ask him."

To them that pray He will give His Divine power.

I went into a community to hold a meeting. They had a magnificent new temple, costing hundreds of thousands of dollars. I got there late to a Monday morning service. A fine crowd was waiting for me at the church. I got off of the train and went to the place I was to stay and then to the church. I went up the steps of the church house, those magnificent stone steps; and there at the top of the steps was a little woman who had on a sunbonnet. She pulled up by the railing and reached out her hand and said, "You are the preacher, are you?" I said, "I am." She said, "I have stopped out here to tell you that we are going to have a great meeting." I looked into her face and saw the expression of earnestness and abiding confidence in God on her face and in her soul. "Well," I said, "that's good news. I would like to know how you know." She said, "For three months, night and day, I have been praying for this meeting and for you and your coming. I have been praying that God would shake this little city in the power of the Divine Spirit. Night by night I have carried this community up to God in prayer and on this morning about five o'clock, by my bedside in prayer, God came and gave me an answer to my prayers. He said, in the secrets of my soul, 'I am going to bless you; and you are going to have a great meeting,' and I have come out here as God's forerunner to tell you that we are going to have a great meeting." I saw the pastor of that church at the close of the meeting baptize hundreds of men and women. And I believe at the judgment bar of God it will be revealed that the one person that did the greatest work of that church was that little woman. We have got to have prayer. The prayer of God's people will avail much to bring down the power of God; and I call everyone of you who believes in Jesus Christ to prayer. I want you to join in the most effective service that can be rendered in this meeting. I ask you if you want God in great power in your community. I ask you to pray; and God help you to pray it through for a great revival of religion.

Now, that is one of the essentials of a great revival. The second essential laid down here is *a
consecrated life.* It is found in the prayer of this
king. He said, "O Lord, remember my life, how
I have lived, how I have walked before thee."
The first thing God's people ought to do to start
a revival is to get right with God and get right
with each other.

In the meeting in which I was converted two of
God's people were at outs with each other. One
was prominent in one church and the other in
another. The preacher preached in the power of
God as I have rarely heard the Gospel preached
for ten days, with no move. But when those two
men got together the power of God broke out on
that city and scores of people were saved. If you
have been doing wrong, you have got to straighten
up. It is a consecrated life that God puts His
blessing on. Ah, there is not anything in this
world aside from the power of God that has in it
the power of the consecrated life. There is nothing in the world like it. Why, the life of your
mother, what a power in bringing you to Jesus
Christ! The life of a consecrated woman lived in
the home with an unsaved man or unsaved children is God's mightiest lever of power in bringing them to Christ. I was in a meeting in Texas
years ago. One morning I said, "I want everyone
of you who was led to Christ by someone in this

audience to go shake hands with that one.'' There
was the pastor who had been there for years.
There were those who could teach and sing and
pray effectively. But I noticed that more than
twenty people went to one simple, plainly dressed
woman. She, they told me, had never prayed in
public, nor taught a Sunday-school class. But she
had more than twenty people to come and shake
hands with her on that proposition. That woman
was the mother of Dr. George Truett.

I heard a man in your town say today, as he
stood by the side of his boy who is a member of
the church, that he was trying to get his boy to
give up some of his pleasures that he ought to
give up. I wonder if that man himself has given
up his sinful ways and is setting the right example before his boy. You have got to clean up if
you are going to have power with God and power
with men. You are going to have to do it. God
help that there shall be tonight and during these
days in your homes and in your private places, a
confession of your sins that God may bring a
great blessing down on your city.

I was holding a meeting. In a great afternoon
service there sat back of me a president of the
great college in that community whose students
by the hundreds were coming to the meeting. He
said to me at the close of the service, ''Do you see
that strong, curly-headed young man standing at
the door?'' I said, ''Yes.'' ''Well,'' he said,
''he is the brightest man in the college, an honor

graduate in this year's class. I have talked with
him and he is a skeptic. He said to me, 'I have
heard this preacher has preached for two weeks.
I have answered every argument he has offered.
In my heart I have answered them all and I do
not believe a thing he has said.' '' The president
said, ''I hope you will try to win him tonight.''
That night I took for my text the prayer of Hezekiah and spoke on the subject, ''The Power of the
Consecrated Life.'' That is the unanswerable
argument. And that night from various angles
I bore down on that crowd. When I gave the
invitation that young man was the first man who
came. He grabbed me by the hand and said, ''I
want to see you.'' I went with him, leaving the
congregation, back into a little room. He sat
there with his big strong body in the chair and
wept for five minutes before he could speak at
all. Then he said, ''You preached for my soul
tonight.'' And then he told me about his skepti-
cism. ''But,'' he said, ''tonight you said, 'There
is some life that is unanswerable.' I want you to
pray for me that I may have what my mother
had.'' He said, ''Three weeks ago when we put
that little body in the ground, that crumpled,
drawn body, I said, 'Something more than human
power made that sweet spirit, that love, something more than that.' '' He said, ''Preacher, I
want what my mother had.'' I tell you that in
less than five minutes he had it. Some years ago
I got off of the train down in Texas and that big

strong man was standing there a high officer in the army. He put his arms around me and said, "I went through the war and all the terrors of the Argonne Forest, and always I felt the power of God around me."

I tell you there is no power like the power of the godly life. What sort of life are you living before your boy? God help you to clean up tonight, that God may have power in this community.

A BURDENED HEART

The third essential is *a burdened heart.* "I have seen thy tears, I have answered thy prayer." The central passion of the gospel is what this city needs tonight. Oh, you have had passion for oil, for making money; you have had that! You have had passion for building a town. I said last night that you could take a little bunch of those men with this spirit and go out here, whether you have oil or not, and build a town. Now, I want you to get a burden for the lost in this city. You have men and women going as straight to hell as these drills out here are going to the bowels of the earth for oil. And you will go on and never shed a tear for the men and women who are going to hell all about you. Why, Jesus Christ spent His life in tears. The Apostle Paul said, "Three and a half years in Ephesus I warned every man with supplication and tears." Somebody has got to weep over this city, or it will go to hell.

"I have seen thy tears." God, as certainly as this city will clean up, will give you a great blessing and you are not going to have it because I am here. I know no tricks of evangelism by which you can build up a revival; but I do know that there is a faith and a prayer that can bring the power of God down; and it is for that that I pray and preach.

Now tonight I want us to put our hands together here on spiritual matters. I have no doubt about your paying the expenses of this meeting; but now, my friends, we are all concerned about the spiritual side of it. Are you going in to bring it about in God's way? I do not want a revival that will leave when I leave. I want your church and all the churches of this city genuinely revived. I want the lost brought to Christ. I love every lost man in this city. I tell you, my friends, God doesn't look at men in the light of how much money they have, or how much oil or leases or royalties they have. God looks at the royalty of the soul. I want to know how many of you want a revival of religion. I am not talking to Baptists alone. How many of you people down in your hearts love Jesus Christ and have trusted Him as your Savior? You may not be a good Christian. But how many of you tonight can say, "Brother Scarborough, down in my soul I do love Jesus Christ?" how many of you who lifted your hands can say, "I want a revival in this town and

I am willing to coöperate in bringing about this revival?''

We have got to meet God's conditions if we have a revival. We have got to pray and straighten up our lives and be burdened for the lost. "They that sow in tears shall reap in joy. He that goeth forth and weepeth, bearing precious seed, shall doubtless come again with rejoicing, bringing his sheaves with him." God help us to go in to win this city for Jesus Christ.

CHAPTER III

COÖPERATION IN SOUL-WINNING

Mark 2:1-12.

I am going to read you about a sick sinner. It is a wonderful story of the power of God.

"And again he entered into Capernaum after some days; and it was noised that he was in the house."

I hope it will get out in this meeting that Jesus Christ is here.

"And straightway many were gathered together, insomuch that there was no room to receive them, no, not so much as about the door: and he preached the word unto them. And they come unto him, bringing one sick of the palsy, which was borne of four. And when they could not come nigh unto him for the press, they uncovered the roof where he was; and when they had broken it up, they let down the bed wherein the sick of the palsy lay. When Jesus saw their faith, he said unto the sick of the palsy, Son, thy sins be forgiven thee. But there were certain of the scribes sitting there, and reasoning in their hearts, Why doth this man thus speak blasphemies? who can forgive sins but God only? And immediately when Jesus perceived in his spirit that they so reasoned within themselves, he said unto them, Why reason ye these things in your hearts? Whether is it easier to say to the sick of the palsy, Thy sins be forgiven thee; or to say, Arise, and take up thy bed, and walk? But that ye may know that the Son of Man hath power on earth to forgive sins (he saith to the sick of the palsy), I say unto thee, Arise, and take up thy bed, and go thy way into thine house. And immediately he arose, took up the bed, and went forth before them all; insomuch that they were all amazed, and glorified God, saying, We never saw it on this fashion.''

This is a very charming story of Christ's coming among the people and the people joining with Christ in bringing the sick and the sinful in touch with His power to heal the sick and to save the lost. There is nowhere in the scriptures a more emphatic and wonderful illustration of two things —the need and the helplessness of the sinner and the incurable disease of sin, and the power of Jesus Christ to forgive sin. There is nowhere a more beautiful example of the spirit of coöperation between God on one side and man on the other in bringing the unsaved in touch with Jesus Christ's power. There was a sick man in Capernaum and some of his friends heard that Jesus, the wonder-worker, was in town. He had come to the town and had stopped at somebody's house. The scriptures do not say whose house it was.

It does not say much about the house, what sort
of furniture was in it, how many people were in
the family. It does not tell how many apartments
in the house, whether the man that owned it had
a big bank account or had no bank account. It
does not say how many oil wells he had or how
many friends he had. But it does say that as soon
as Christ got to town He went to this man's house.
He made a welcome for Jesus Christ, and not only
did he make a welcome for Jesus Christ, but he
made a welcome for the sick, unsaved man. Why,
he went so far as to let them take the roof off of
his house because that roof stood in the way of
getting a lost man to Jesus Christ. I trust that
there are none of you business men who will let
your business get in the way of lost souls in this
meeting. I trust that none of you women who
love God will let the domestic affairs of your
home get in the way of lost people coming to
Jesus Christ and of your doing your duty to God.
I wonder how many there are of God's people in
this coöperating little city who are willing to
make the salvation of men the main thing for
these two weeks, setting aside your business, if
need be, setting aside the concerns of your lives
if need be, in order to bring your unsaved friends
to Jesus Christ and to set the right sort of an example for them in taking part in Christ's religion. The names of these four men are not
given. Nothing is said about them as to their
business or how long they had been Christians.

It is only said that they went to the house of this man, this paralyzed man, this man who had an incurable disease, this helpless sinner, and by the strength of their bodies and the willingness of their souls, in coöperation together, they brought this man in touch with the power of Jesus Christ. I am sure that this man long remembered these four men. Oh, I bless God tonight for the people that brought me to Jesus Christ. Last night, and probably here tonight, is the man who when I was a schoolboy, excused me from my classes that I might go down to the church one morning where an evangelistic service was going on. All these years, though I have seen him but few times since then, I have blessed God for that faithful, consecrated, Christian teacher—Prof. Witt—who had something to do with bringing me to Jesus Christ. I bless God for my mother and my father and that dear old deacon in that church and the pastor's wife in that church, who brought me to Jesus Christ and had something to do with getting me in touch with the Divine Power.

These four men in this beautiful story had courage. They had faith. They knew the power of God. They loved this helpless, lost, unsaved man and they went to inconvenience and crossed the currents of men's opinions in order to get this man to Jesus Christ. I can see them now coming down the street of Capernaum, one at either corner of that couch. I can see them as they left his home. His wife I judge had for many years cared for her husband, had gotten every doctor that she thought could help him. I can see her that night when these four men knocked at her door and said, "We have come for your husband. The Healer is in town and we are going to carry him where he can be healed of this paralysis, this incurable disease." I can see her as she helped to put him on the couch and as they took him down the street and as they got to the door and could not get in, as they climbed up the stairway and went onto the top of the house. I can see them now as they laid him down on the roof, tore up the tiling—the roof of the house. I can see them as they let him down into the presence of Jesus Christ. I can see them as they stretched themselves out on the roof and looked down at Jesus as He spoke the life-giving, healing words. I can see them now as Jesus looked up into their faces and spoke to them when He saw their faith. Thank God, it does not say when He saw their clothes, nor when He saw their bank account, nor when He saw their education, nor standing, nor prestige in the community, but when He saw their faith. It was on the faith of those four men and on the faith of this paralyzed man that lay at His feet that Jesus Christ spoke the life-giving words. I wonder who is going to have that faith in this meeting tonight, and during these days, seeing whose faith Jesus Christ will say, "Son, thy sins be forgiven thee."

I will tell you, my friends, there is an opportu-

nity for every child of God to render invaluable
service to this meeting. You may not speak a
word, you may not sing the verse of a song, you
may not pray a public prayer; but if in your heart
there is faith, conquering faith in Jesus Christ
and you bring His power here, I will tell you you
will be more valuable than the preacher and more
valuable than the singer. God help you tonight
to function at the place where you can function,
and that is faith in Jesus Christ.

I can hear Him now, the Son of man Who hath
power on earth to forgive sins, looking down into
the face of that paralyzed sinner, and I bless God
that He saved his soul before He healed his body.
Christ thus put His Divine emphasis and the
mighty example of His power upon the fact that
the saving of the soul is worth a great deal more
than the healing of the body. He makes the salvation of the soul the main thing and the best thing.
I can hear Him now, I did hear Him thirty-six
years ago when He looked into my soul and said,
"Son, thy sins be forgiven thee." Oh, how I bless
God for the hour when Jesus spoke to my soul and
forgave my sins and reached down His redeeming,
saving hand and took me up out of the miry clay
and redeemed my spirit and put a new song into
my soul, a new power into my life. I thank God
for that power He has on earth to forgive the sins
of men. I can see now that man saved by the
grace of God, yet paralyzed in his body, and Jesus
saying, "Take up thy bed and go thy way." Oh,

I bless God that Jesus has power over the diseases of men. I do not believe that men ought to deny the power of medicine; but I do believe that Jesus Christ has power today over the diseases that come to our bodies. When my people get sick I send for two doctors. I send for the doctor that knows how to administer medicine and I, by prayer, send for the Doctor that knows how to take care of the medical doctors.

THE PARALYZED SINNER

I want you tonight to look at this unsaved man, this paralyzed man, because it is Christ's outstanding example of the condition of a sinner. I tell you tonight, my friends, if you have not trusted in Jesus Christ as your personal Savior, you have a spiritual paralysis that nothing but Jesus Christ can cure. And this man is but God's picture of the paralysis of your soul. There is no doctor that can cure paralysis.

I am thinking now of my brother, a big, strong man weighing over 315 pounds. I remember when I was in a meeting they phoned me that he was stricken with paralysis and for four or five years I took him to many doctors trying to find somebody that had the skill and power to stop that awful disease. Every doctor that we went to, when he examined him shook his head and said, "I know no remedy."

Oh, my friends, if there is an unsaved man here, without Jesus Christ, you have a paralysis that nobody and nothing can cure besides the blood and the righteousness of Jesus Christ. The sinner before God is a paralyzed man. Sin is the most awful disease that ever took hold on man. I know typhoid fever is bad; I know that paralysis is bad; I know that the white plague—tuberculosis—is bad. I know that there are other dreadful diseases; but, my friends, there is more danger done and more ruin wrought by sin than by all the other diseases of the world. And tonight sin is in your soul, in every particle of your being, in your eternal spirit. And the wrath of God is on you. Oh, how awful is the paralysis of the soul! And tonight in this picture there is the photograph of your own case, my friends, if you have never trusted in Jesus Christ.

THE SINNER IS HELPLESS

Not only did this man have an incurable disease, but he was helpless. And so is every unsaved man absolutely helpless. Why, he is blind; he is blind to spiritual things; he is blind to God; he is blind to spiritual life; he is dead in trespasses and in sins. The very wrath of God is on him and he is helpless. Oh, my friends, my Christian friends, tonight I wish that we could realize the helplessness of the unsaved here.

I was in a meeting. An unsaved man in the back of the house lifted his hand. The pastor went and spoke to him. The next night the man came again. At the close of the service he stood up. The pastor spoke to him again. The next night that man came down to the front and gave me his hand. He made an impression on my soul. The next afternoon I was in the pastor's study getting ready for the evening service. There was a knock on the door. I opened the door. There walked in this man. He sat in the seat that I offered him. I had my Bible in my hand. I said, "My friend, what can I do for you?" He said, "I do not know why I came here." I said, "You are the man that has been seeking Christ in these meetings and God has led you here that I might help you to find Christ." He looked me in the face and said, "I am 60 years of age and for thirty years I have been not only an infidel but an atheist. I do not believe in Jesus Christ. I neither believe that He was the Son of God, nor the Son of Mary. I believe the whole story is the product of an inflamed imagination and that there was no such person as Jesus Christ." He took the Bible out of my hand. He said, "For thirty years I have denied this book's divinity. I have taken it leaf by leaf and page by page and torn it into a thousand tatters and jumped on it with my feet and said, 'It is an old woman's lie!'" Said he, "I do not believe in the inspiration of this book." He tried to take from me my Christ. He tried to take from me my Bible. I looked into his face. The tears were coming down his cheeks. I said, "You do not believe in God. You do not believe in the Bible. Do you believe that you are a sinner?" And, with a trembling voice, he said, "I know I am a sinner." "Then," I said, "my friend, I know I have a Savior. Let's pray." And in each others arms, mine around him and his arms about me, we went to our knees. I never before realized how helpless is an unsaved man and how helpless is the child of God in the presence of an unbelieving sinner. I took that man in the arms of faith and love, remembering that the blood of Jesus Christ can cleanse from all sin, and I carried him up to Jesus Christ and laid him down at the feet of the Savior. I had not finished the prayer until he leaped from his knees and said, "I have found Him and He is mine. I deny the denials of thirty years. Jesus Christ is real to me." He took my Bible and hugged it to his bosom and said, "I believe every word of it." I have come from that incident remembering that unsaved men are helpless men and that somebody must bring them to Jesus Christ.

COÖPERATION IN SOUL-WINNING

I want you to look from this unsaved, helpless man who had an incurable disease to these four men. What a beautiful example for us of coöperation; and in what follows now tonight I am going to show every man and woman that loves Jesus Christ how you can bring someone to Jesus Christ. What did these men do?

The first thing they did, they *planned* to bring him to Jesus. I can see them now. One man in the streets of Capernaum, keeping a corner store, walked across the street to another man's place of business and said, "Our paralyzed friend needs somebody to carry him down to the house of Brother So and So where Jesus is going to speak." He said, "Why, we cannot carry him." The first man said, "We will get somebody to help us." They went together to Brother So and So and said, "We want you to help us." And then they went across the street to a fourth man and said, "We want you to help us." And that night at the appointed hour they were down at the house of the helpless man. They planned to bring him to Christ.

Yonder in the city of Waco Dr. Carroll was holding a great meeting. It went on for ten or twelve weeks. It was one of the greatest meetings ever held in any part of Texas. One night, as I have been told out of that great audience, a deacon stopped at the door and as the other deacons, five of them, passed out he called them into a little room. As they sat in that room he spoke to them about Judge So and So, a prominent lawyer who was a state-wide and a nation-wide infidel, and said to those deacons, "He is on my heart." They said, "Let's win him to Christ." There they planned it. Next morning one of them went into the Judge's office and said a few words to him about the meeting and said, "Six of us are praying for your soul." At 9:30 another man went into the office and said about the same thing

and as he started out this Judge said, "You are
the second man that has been here this morning.
What is the matter with me?" The deacon went
his way. At 10 o'clock another man came in and
said about the same thing. By this time the Judge
was aroused. He said, "Am I murderer; what
have I done; what crime have I committed that
you Baptist people are coming here?" He went
his way. At 10:30 another came and said about
the same thing. At 11 o'clock another came. At
11:30 another, the sixth one of the deacons, came
into that office and that Judge promised to be at
church that night and on the third night he and
six others, all leading infidels, came and gave
their hearts to Christ and joined the church. It
was because somebody planned to bring him to
Christ. Oh, I thank God for the people who plan
to bring others to Christ. I want you men, you
women, you are thinking of somebody now that
you would like to see saved, I want you to make
plans in your souls by which you will try to lead
them to Christ. It is letting people alone that
sends them to hell. It is planning to go after
them that brings them to Jesus Christ. Plan to
bring them to Christ.

But these men not only planned it, they *pushed
their plans.* They did not stop with praying; they
did not stop with planning. Some man today
called up and said, "I want the names of unsaved
men." And when he was questioned about it, he
said, "I want to pray for them." I bless God for

the people who are going to pray for the unsaved men; but I want you to plan for their salvation and push your plans and go after them for Jesus Christ. These men were willing to face difficulties and criticism and ride over their difficulties and tear off the roof of a man's house, willing to do anything in order to push their plans. God help you to have the same courage and the same interest. God help you to make plans in bringing your friends to Jesus Christ. Oh, how many men go down to hell because nobody cares for them, nobody sees after them.

Some years ago on one journey I traveled 8,000 miles, visiting nearly every State of the Union. I was in churches, I was in banks, I was in sleeping cars, in smoking cars, on chair cars. I was in Sunday-school classes. I was on the streets of some of our largest cities. I was in villages and towns. I was in the country. And in that journey of 8,000 miles I saw preachers and Sunday school teachers. I saw deacons. I saw all sorts of men. And yet, only one man in a journey of 8,000 miles spoke to me about my soul. I was on hundreds of trains anyone of which falling into a ditch might have sent my soul into eternity.

Oh, my friends, I want you to coöperate in bringing somebody to Jesus Christ. I do not want to meet anybody at the Judgment whose blood is on my hands. God help you tonight to know that if you do not do your duty to the unsaved that God has selected for you to win to

Christ, in all probability nobody else will reach them. And they may go down to hell leaving their blood on your hands.

These four men brought their friend to Jesus and Jesus did the rest. I can see those four men now up on that roof. They have seen him get up. They have seen his smiling face when Jesus saved his soul. They saw his leaping body as he was cured of the disease. They saw him as he took his bed and made for the door. I can see them now going down the stairway. And on the outside, meeting the healed, saved sinner, I can see them rejoicing now. And they could say to Jesus, "We did it. We brought him and you saved him and healed him. We did all we could." I can see them carrying that man home and when he gets to the door and they tell his wife, "Your husband is healed. Your husband is saved," I know there was an old time camp-meeting in that house that night. Oh, my friends, there ought to be a hundred homes in this city rejoicing when your friends find Jesus Christ. I will do you an injustice if I win all the people to Christ that are won to Him in this meeting. I want it to be your meeting. I do not want to be the spiritual father of all the saved in this meeting. I want them to be your spiritual children and then you will take care of them. God help us to coöperate with Christ in bringing our friends to Him.

Now, the best thing about this story in this wonderful text is Jesus. Thank God, He comes down

among the people. "It was noised that He was
in the house." Oh, my friends, Lee Scarborough
cannot hold a meeting and the pastor of this
church cannot hold a meeting. All these preachers and singers cannot have a genuine revival in
our own strength. But, thank God, if we get Jesus
Christ here there are not devils enough in hell to
keep us from having a meeting. Let us get Him.
He is risen from the dead. He is the living Son
of God; and tonight He sits regnant on the throne.
Oh, my unsaved friend, He has power on earth to
forgive sin. I send out the word to every sinner
that Jesus Christ has power on earth to save
souls. Let us, let all the people of this flourishing
little city know that Jesus Christ has power on
earth to forgive sins; and He can save and save
now.

CHAPTER IV

IT WAS NOISED THAT HE WAS IN THE HOUSE

Mark 2:1-12.

Last evening I spoke to you on that wonderful miracle of our Savior where He healed and saved the paralyzed man. This morning I wish to speak upon one clause in the introduction to this parable: "It was noised that He was in the house."

Christ had been out about Capernaum teaching and healing and preaching the Gospel. There was somebody's house in Capernaum to which He delighted to go. I do not know what it is about a home that attracts Christ. I wonder if you have that secret in your home. Suppose Jesus Christ this morning were to get off of one of your passenger trains, or suppose He were to come by someone of His heavenly aeroplanes and stop in your city. I wonder whose home He would visit first. What is there in your home that would attract Him or repel Him? There was something in this home in Capernaum that attracted the Son of Man. As I said last night, that man made a welcome for Christ, made a hospital for the sick, and a house of repentance and salvation for the lost. Now, "It was noised that He was in the

house." Notice what happened when it got out
that Jesus was in this house. They immediately
arranged to hear Him. The crowd was attracted.
The needy came. The lost were brought. Great
power came. Healing came; salvation came.
These are some of the things that go where Christ
goes. Now, I bless God that this incident in the
earthly ministry of Christ is but an example to
show us the habits of Jesus Christ. I bless God
that He delights to come among His people. So
many times in His earthly ministry He found the
people.

He found the woman at the well side and saved
her, the big man in the upper room and saved him.
He found blind Bartimæus sitting by the roadside, called him and gave him his sight and salvation. He found the man of small stature, who,
because of his enthusiasm to see Jesus Christ,
climbed up a tree, and the Savior called him down
and went to his house and saved him. And after
His resurrection He appeared to His people. On
one occasion by the side of the open grave which
His power had emptied He spoke to the women
and delivered a message. On one occasion by the
roadside as two of His disciples were on their
way to Emmaus He appeared among them and
their hearts burned within them as He opened to
them the scriptures. On one occasion when the
disciples, for fear of the Jews, were locked within
a small room through the barred doors Jesus came
in His resurrection body and breathed on them

and gave them peace and bade them receive the
Holy Spirit, and delivered unto them the commis-
sion: "As my father hath sent me into the world
so also I send you into the world." He appeared
to Peter. He appeared to the two disciples. He
appeared to five hundred of the disciples. I thank
God today, my friends, that it is the habit of Jesus
Christ to come among His people. These are the
records of old; but I bless God that each one of
us who loves the Savior can testify to many occa-
sions on which He came when we prayed, when
we talked together about Him, when we were in
sorrow, when we faced some great task, when some
great temptation came. I bless His holy name
that in this modern day there are demonstrations
of the fact that Jesus Christ appears among His
people. "It was noised that He was in the
house." It was Christ that was the attraction on
that occasion. They came to hear Him. They
came to see His power. They brought their
friends that His healing and saving power might
operate on the needy. Jesus Christ was the center of that great, miraculous, saving evangelism
in that day.

HE IS THE ONE ESSENTIAL

I wish to say to you this morning that our one
necessity is Jesus Christ. We can get along without everything else but Him. We do not have to
have a great church or a well built tabernacle.
We can get along without a singer. We can get

along without a choir. We can get along without preachers, but we cannot get along without Jesus.

I think the greatest meeting I ever saw was under the shade of a big elm tree on the Clear Fork of the Brazos River in West Texas, forty years ago. There was not a chair for anybody to sit on. There was but one song book; there was but one preacher; there was but one Bible. At no time during that meeting were there as many present as there are here this morning; and yet out of that meeting grew many of the strongest churches of West Texas. In that meeting this unworthy servant, a lad of eleven years of age, got his first conception of the gospel and the first sense that he ever had of the value of spiritual things. I will tell you, my friends, in the midst of that little meeting in West Texas, forty years ago, there stood a reigning, ruling, regnant Christ.

I say you can get along without preachers. In the mountains of North Carolina, I am told, in a little country church, having once-per-month preaching, they set a time far ahead for their summer meeting. They were to begin on Saturday morning. The preacher lived forty miles away and had to cross the mountains and the streams for forty miles to get to his appointment. Twenty members of the church on Saturday morning met. No preacher came. They said, "He will be here tonight. The streams are swollen, but he will be here tonight." They held a service and came back that night, still no preacher came. They said, "He

was delayed by the swollen streams and will be
here tomorrow." They came again on Sunday
morning. Still no preacher came. They held a
service. Sunday night there was still no preacher,
but they held a service. That meeting went on
for ten days and no preacher came during the
meeting. But when the preacher did come each
one of the members of that church had six apiece
ready for baptism—one hundred and twenty.
There was not a preacher in forty miles of that
meeting, but they had Jesus Christ. They prayed;
they testified; they sang and read the scriptures,
and God's power came.

My friends, Jesus Christ is the one necessity of
every revival.

I had an engagement recently in one of our college towns. There were five or six hundred students and I was to hold a meeting with the church
nearest to the college. They said in their letter,
"We have searched the world and have decided
that you are God's man and the only man that
we know that God has that can reach us in a great
revival." I accepted the invitation, and, as I
thought, the appointment of God. Ten days before the time I was to go I had to set aside all
my engagements and give two months of my time
to the Seventy-five Million Campaign this last
spring. I wired the pastor that I could not come.
He wired back and said, "It is absolutely neces-
sary that you come. We cannot get along without
you." I wired back, "No, you have only one

necessity and that is Jesus Christ. You get in
with Him and go on with the meeting.'' The pastor took up the meeting. They got in with Jesus
Christ and baptized a large number of those students and other people around, and wrote me after
the meeting and said, ''Thank God, you are not a
necessity for a revival, but Jesus Christ is.'' I
bless God that Jesus Christ is in reach of every
group of His disciples and He will come, and when
He comes we have all we need.

THE BASIS ON WHICH HE COMES

What is the basis on which Jesus Christ comes
among His people, to the individual heart, to the
group of His people? What is the basis? On
what condition will He come? I wish to say in the
first place that Jesus Christ comes into a community and blesses His people on the basis of their
consecrated lives. My friends, I do not believe
that there is any merit in our lives as to our salvation; but there is merit in our lives as to our
power. On the basis of righteousness Jesus Christ
comes into a community and blesses it. You need
not expect that Jesus Christ is going to give you
a personal blessing so long as you are living rag-
ged and godless lives.

I went into a community once where the pastor
said to me, ''We have made fine preparation for
a meeting. We have turned out fifty-seven.'' I
said, ''You have already had a back-door revival.'' He said, ''The bunch that is here now

are cleaned up and we believe we have a consecrated crowd to put over our meeting." I saw
that pastor baptize sixty-seven grown men at one
afternoon service. No wonder they had the power
of God! They had cleaned up their lives. Now,
you need not think, my brother, that God is going
to come in and bless you and give you His power
as long as you run with the hare and the hounds.
I tell you, so many of our churches have so many
godless people in them, people who lie and swear
and take everything into their lives except God,
and yet they carry around the plates and take up
the collections—some of them—and sometimes
they carry around the holy bread of the Lord's
Supper, and they go on with the devil in their lives
trying to bring the power of God into the community; and the church is helpless and nobody
can have the power of God, because they block the
power of God. Now, we have got to clean up if
we have Jesus Christ to come into our midst.

In one of the first meetings I ever held in a
country church I preached ten days, staying in
the home of a brother who was the gin man in
the community. And the gin man is always a
very important person in the country communi-
ties. He was a member of the Baptist church in
that community. There was a steward in the
Methodist church that was also a prominent man
in the community. And they would not speak to
each other. And there was a prominent elder in
the Presbyterian church that would not speak to

either of these. And there was a three-cornered
row. I did not know anything about it. They all
came to church. One day, after ten days' preaching and no move had been made, I was sitting in
the home of this brother with whom I was staying. I turned to him and said, "C. B., there is
something wrong in this community, something
'rotten in Denmark,' something wrong in the lives
of some of these people." I noticed a tear gather
in his eyes. I said, "Somebody is wrong; there
is unforgiveness, there is trouble between somebody in this community." I was guessing. I saw
tears come into his eyes as he said, "Brother, I
am blocking this meeting." He said, "There are
two men that sit in that church I will not speak
to and they wont speak to me." That morning
in the service, when the house was packed with
people, I preached on "Unforgiveness." I started away over yonder and came up a little closer
and a little closer and a little closer and by and by
I got down to where I said, "Thou art the man."
While I was preaching, by the power of God, almost at the same time, those three men got up
and made for each other. The brother with whom
I was staying weighed about three hundred
pounds, the Methodist steward weighed something
like two hundred and fifty pounds and the Presbyterian brother weighed something like two hundred pounds. They looked like elephants as they
came together. And the aisle was too narrow for
them to hug. I brought them in to the altar and

we had a three-cornered hugging. I never saw such making up. While they had charge of the meeting I saw fourteen men give their hearts to Jesus Christ. Jesus Christ could not come into that community until those men got right.

I do not know whether there is anything in this community like that or not; but the people of God to have the power of God must clean up their lives.

Now, there is another basis on which Jesus Christ comes. He comes into a community on the basis of the *faith of the people,* their confidence in Him, their belief in Him, their faith in the power of His Gospel, their confidence in its saving, reviving power. Jesus Christ could do no mighty works in Nazareth because of their unbelief. Why, in this very story there were scribes sitting there reasoning in their hearts, raising questions as to whether or not Jesus had power on earth to forgive sins and Jesus Christ could not do anything with those people. It was the faith of those four men that moved the arm of Jesus Christ. Somebody must have faith and confidence in order to have God to make a demonstration of power. I ask you do you believe in the power of Jesus Christ to save and to heal and to revive. That is a condition of a revival. "It was noised that He was in the house." Somebody believed in Him and He went where there was faith. I will tell you, my friends, somebody has got to believe in God. "Whatsoever things ye desire when, ye pray, believe that ye have them and ye shall have them," is the eternal promise of God. It is on the basis of the faith of God's people that He comes.

There is another basis and that is a basis of *love,* personal affection for Jesus Christ. It is a love that will share no honor with anybody else, a love supreme for Christ. It is a love that in the balance with other things will outweigh for Jesus Christ. I wonder how much we love Him. Do we love Him more than we love our oil wells, or our royalties, or our household affairs, or our business, or our pleasure, or our loved ones? Do we love Jesus Christ supremely? It is on that basis that Jesus Christ comes into a community. He will not share His love with anything else. I tell you, the trouble with some people is like the trouble with the little girl, who went into the parlor and climbed into a chair by the center table and took off of the table a vase. She looked into the vase and saw at the bottom of it a nickel. She ran her little hand into the vase and closed it over the nickel, and then tried to pull her hand out of the vase. When her hand would not come out she called her mother. Her mother could not get the vase off of the hand. She called the little girl's father. He came and tried to get it off. Finally he said, "Mary, you open your hand like Daddy's and draw your hand out." She looked up and said, "Daddy, if I do I will drop the nickel." The trouble with some people is they are holding on to something that they do not want to give up. I will tell you, my friends, if we are to have power from Almighty God we have got to love Jesus Christ supremely.

There is another basis on which Jesus Christ comes into a community and that is the basis of *service,* of coöperation, of willingness to do His will, of a surrendered life to Him. My brethren, we will never know how much power with Jesus Christ these four men had that brought this paralyzed man to Jesus. There was coöperation. There was service. And when they came with their faith and showed their faith by their works, Jesus Christ exercised His power. I want to say to you that one of the conditions of a revival in this city is that God's people will be willing to do the will of God at any cost. Now, there are a good many things I do not know; but there are some things I do know from the Word of God and from twenty-five years' experience as a minister. I never saw a more beautiful spirit of coöperation in all the material things than I see in connection with this meeting—in building this tabernacle, in advertising the meeting, and so on and so on. Now, we have come to the final question, as to whether or not you are going to coöperate in the spiritual matter, the main matter. Are you willing to serve? Are you willing to do His will?

I was in a meeting. I got there on Monday morning. We had a great service. After the service a beautiful young woman, a member of the graduating class at Baylor University, a cultured, refined young woman came up to me. Her father was an unsaved, wealthy farmer. Her mother and sister and she were Christians. She said to me, "Brother Scarborough, Mother and Sister and I have been praying for months about your coming. Our father has great confidence in you and you are the only preacher in all this country in which he does have any confidence. And we believe that God will use you to bring him to Jesus Christ." I do not know why I asked her the question, but I did. I said, "Miss Minnie, are you willing to do the will of God?" I touched a tender spot. It developed that she was called to be a missionary and for twelve months she had been fighting that call. I said, "Are you willing to do the will of God?" She broke down and sat on the front seat in front of me and did not answer. I pressed the question. Every time I asked her it would bring new expressions of emotion to her face. I said, "Miss Minnie, I can pray for and preach to and use my influence with your father; but I am afraid if there is rebellion in his family, I am afraid you will block the power of God." I said, "Are you willing to do the will of God?" I said, "You are called to be a missionary." She said, "I am." I said, "Are you willing to surrender in order that your father may be brought to Jesus Christ?" She went through that meeting a rebellious child of God. Her father went through the meeting unsaved. Four years after

that he died and went into eternity; and that girl
is living a rebellious life today. Service and willingness to serve Jesus Christ are the basis on
which He gives His power and comes into a community.

Oh, my friends, there is great interest here on
the part of the unsaved. One man here Sunday
night had not heard a sermon in twenty-four
years. One last night said, "My mother yonder
in Mangum heard you preach twelve years ago
and she wrote me and said, 'By all means go to
hear him preach.' I thank God though he was unsaved when he came into this tabernacle he was a
saved man before he got away. Another man in
the audience last night said, "I hate to leave this
town. I am lost." All over this community there
are people concerned about their souls' salvation.
I wonder if this group of God's people are willing
to do the will of God. I will tell you, my friends,
when Jesus Christ comes into a community it
makes all the difference in the world. He changes
things when He comes. There is no trouble
about the crowds, there is no trouble about the
coöperation, there is no trouble about the power
and the grace of God, when it gets out that Jesus
is in the crowd.

CHAPTER V

GOING DEEPER WITH GOD

In the 47th chapter of Ezekiel an angel was sent to the prophet with a measuring line in his hands and he says:

"And when the man that had the line in his hand went forth eastward, he measured a thousand cubits, and he brought me through the waters; the waters were to the ankles. Again he measured a thousand, and brought me through the waters; the waters were to the knees. Again he measured a thousand, and brought me through; the waters were to the loins. Afterward he measured a thousand; and it was a river that I could not pass over: for the waters were risen, waters to swim in, a river that could not be passed over."

That is a picture of the different kinds of Christians. Some are into Christianity ankle deep, some knee deep, some loin deep; and some, thank God, have thoroughly surrendered themselves to the service of God and they are out in the waters —waters to swim in, in the impassable and glorious seas and tides of God's power and love and grace and strength.

In John, the 10th chapter and the 10th verse, Jesus says:

"The thief cometh not, but for to steal, and to kill, and to destroy: I come that they might have life, and that they might have it more abundantly."

And in John the 7th chapter and 38th verse, He says:

"He that believeth on me, as the scripture hath said, from within him shall flow rivers of living water."

I saw in the paper, last night I think it was, where a man out here bored a well for oil and went down about 1,800 feet, I think, but struck a little oil but the water got into it and it quit flowing. He went down a little further some time after that, thought he had a bad well. He went over 2,000 feet and something happened and it looked like he did not have a good well. But he went down yesterday, and swabbed it out and cleaned it out and the paper says it now looks like it is a 1,000 or 1,500-barrel well. He went deeper.

In the days of gold in California a man who had a fortune bought a piece of land in the gold fields and sank a shaft and went down and down but struck no gold. He spent his fortune on an empty shaft. He was a Christian man. One night in a dream he dreamed that God came and said to him, "Go deeper." Taking the intimation and suggestion from that dream as a divine call, he went east and borrowed a fortune and put it into that shaft and went deeper and deeper. He spent that fortune and found no gold. God came to him in another dream and said, "Go deeper." He followed what he regarded as a divine impression and borrowed another fortune and went deeper and deeper and finally he found an almost inexhaustible supply of gold, paid back the two fortunes he had borrowed, recouped himself of the fortune he himself had lost and then had large money. One night God came to him in another dream and added a word to the other that He had given him and in that dream He said, "Go deeper with God; go deeper with God." That man then began to spend his money, not for luxury and travel and pleasure and selfish indulgences, but he began to spend it for God in the building of orphanages, in the building of hospitals, in the building of church houses and schools, in the spreading of the Gospel of Jesus Christ. He went deeper with God.

THE SIN OF SHALLOWNESS

I will tell you, my friends, the saddest thing I know today of our Christianity is that it is so shallow. It is not deep. It does not go down to the roots of things. We do not give attention to the fountains of spiritual life and power just beneath. It takes digging and drilling. It takes interest and service and prayer and faith to go

deeper with God. I will tell you, my friends, today one of the saddest things in this world is that
you and I are so easily swept off of our feet by
temptations, by adversities, by prosperity, by
sickness, or by health. Now we need to go deeper
with God. I wish to speak to you this morning
about the deeper life with God.

I was in Roswell, New Mexico, some time ago
in a great meeting. One morning my friends came
early in their automobile and said, ''We want to
show you the city and the valley and the sources
of our wealth and joy in this little western city
of the plains.'' They drove me down that beautiful valley. It is one of the luxurious spots of the
earth. Beautiful trees come up from the side of
the lane where the irrigating canals run. On
every side are the alfalfa fields and orchards.
The land is worth from four to five hundred dollars an acre. Everywhere there was beauty and
joy and luxury as the irrigating canals carried
the fresh life-giving waters to the earth. They
took me through the beautiful little city and to
the beautiful lake. The lake had no trees about
it. It had no inlet. The water was not running
into that lake where you could see it. But from
the lake the water ran off down into what they
call Spring Creek. That lake is supplied, they
tell me, from inner fountains that live at the root
of the Rocky Mountains which you can see in the
distance. And that little stream runs through the

beautiful little city of Roswell. On the other side of the city is another stream—Hondo. It rises in the mountains. That stream does not have any water in it except in the time of the rains and when the spring warmth comes and warms the snow of the mountains. Then it comes with a mighty flooding tide. The rest of the time it is dry. Land on Hondo is worth $3 an acre. I said, as they told me that story, ''That is the picture of Christians. There are Christians who have a steady flow of life and power and influence; constantly during the years their life is flowing out and blessing other lives. Everywhere you can always count on them. They are in their places in the service of God, in the prayer-meeting, in the Sunday-night services, and in the other services of the house of God. They live on Spring Creek. They are in constant connection with the eternal fountain—Jesus Christ—and from within them flow rivers of living water. I am speaking now of the Christians that have gone down beyond ankle deep and they are out in God's stream of life and power and they have joy and peace.

There is another kind of Christian. There is the one that comes in during the big meeting. They get their hearts warmed and for a few days they walk an upright life. And then after the big meeting goes, they drift away. They complain if they have to give a little money; they are not prayerful; they do not study the Bible. They are saved, perhaps, but they live on Hondo. There are no springs of life and joy and power in their hearts.

THE DEEPER LIFE

I would speak to you a message that would call you back to the deeper life, the steadier life, the life of joy and power in the service of God. Jesus said, "I came that they may have life," yes, life eternal, life that saves, life with God, life in peace and harmony with the Divine. But He said, "I came that they may have the abundant life, the life that overflows, that has joy and power and peace, the overflowing life with Jesus Christ. Every child of God has a claim on and a right to the deeper life with Jesus Christ.

I had a letter yesterday from a woman who lives in Oakland, California. I was her pastor for seven years. She did not have a college education. Her husband was a farmer. They had moved to town to educate their children. That woman lived in the church where I was pastor for seven years and I wish to thank God for that Christian woman. Oh, the poor people in the winter time that she clothed and fed and got wood and coal and fire and warmth for! Oh, the unsaved people that, during the revivals and between time, she talked to about Jesus Christ! Oh, the sick people to whom she carried flowers and meals! Oh, the life, the glorious, triumphant life she lived and lives today! I bless God for such a life.

I would call you this morning out of your sins, out of your littleness, out of your meanness, out of that shallow life you are living, into a deeper life with God, a life that overflows, in the times of adversity as well as in the times of prosperity—a life that can sing about the sick bed and have the joy bells ringing in your heart when the crêpe is on the door. It is in reach of every child of God.

ESSENTIALS TO THE DEEPER LIFE

There are some things that are essential to this life, if we are to have it.

In the first place, we must be *separated from our sins.* There must be a separation from sin if there is to be a deeper life with God. You cannot run with the hare and the hounds and ever catch the hare. You cannot go along in your old sinful way and have joy and peace and power with God. One of the things you need is cleaning up. You women that are going around members of churches and finding no pleasure except in the card party and in the moving-picture show and in the dance, you need a cleaning up in your lives. You men that are grafters, I tell you there are people in this town who ought to lower the rents for the good people who live here. I will tell you, my friends, your grafting is not a product of Christianity. Oh, you say, "Others are doing it." God help you, that is no reason why you as a saved man should do the same thing. I have just heard of one man in the oil fields who, when the oil fever came on in his town, raised his rent just a little bit. Right across the street from one of his houses was a house rented for $150 a month. He rented his house, a better house, for $40 a month and he said, "I am not going to graft on the poor people of this community." A man in this town wrote me a note. I do not know who it was. And he said, "There are some people in this town of your cult, if they would change their rentals some of us would have more interest in the golden gates and pearly streets up yonder."

We are not going to live the deeper life with God and go on like the sins of the world go. God help your Christianity to clean up and get on the high road for Jesus Christ.

There is another essential and that is *consecration*, not only separation, but consecration to the service of God. I thank God today that there are men, strong, virile, vigorous men that are prospering and making money and they are not doing it by grafting, but they are devoted to the service of Jesus Christ, and we need more of them. Oh, my friends, I know what the appeal of this world is. For eight long years I had an ambition to be a lawyer. I studied to be a lawyer. I wanted the fine house and the big bank account and the big reputation. I know what that appeal is; but I thank God that yonder in old Farnum Hall at Yale University, some twenty-five years ago, Jesus Christ came and put to death in my heart and in my life the ambition for that sort of thing.

I will tell you you have got to have a consecration
of your talents and your powers to the service of
God.

A beautiful young woman was preparing her-
self for operatic singing. She was a professed
Christian, not living very much in that line,
though. In a meeting, a great crowd of some
2,500 people, she was asked to sing and she sang
beautifully. When she turned around to sit on
the platform behind me, I took her by the hand
and I said, ''Young woman, if that voice of yours
were consecrated to the service of God you could
do a mighty work for the Master.'' It stuck in
her heart. Next morning I had a telephone call
from her. She said, ''I want to see you. I want
to talk with you. I could not sleep last night.''
She said before I left her, ''I will give my life
and my voice to Jesus Christ.'' That night she
sang and as she got up to sing, I said, ''Last night
she sang for the admiration of men, but tonight
she sings for the glory of Jesus Christ.'' And
soon after she sang I saw a number of grown people give their hearts to Christ. We need to devote
our talents and our time to the service of God if
we are going to go deeper with God.

There is another essential in this matter of going deeper with God and that is *communion—
prayer*. You cannot go deeper with God and live
a prayerless life. Oh, how our people are prayerless. We pay our pastor to preach for us and

most people seem to pay him to do their praying
for them.

In my pastorate I went to a big fine man and
asked him to do something. He said, "No, I am
paying you to do that." Most people today pay
the preacher and let him do their praying. You
cannot live and get along on warmed over bread.
You have got to go to God yourself and pray and
get fellowship with Him. Oh, the man or the
woman who is in constant communion and touch
and power with God is going to go deeper with
God.

There is another essential in this matter of going deeper with God and that is *information*, not
only separation from sin and consecration to the
service of God and communion with Jesus Christ,
but information about God. How few people
there are who study the Word of God today. I
can submit to a test the Christians of this audience and how few of you can name the books of
the Bible and how few of you know many of the
promises of God. I could get testimonies of books
not in the Bible at all. I asked the superintendent
of a Sunday school and others recently if the book
of Hezekiah is in the Old Testament or the New
Testament. And about a dozen hands went up
testifying that it is in the Old Testament. Oh,
the ignorance of God's Word is appalling. How
little we know about the Bible! You cannot go
deep with God and neglect this old Book. There
are fountains of life and power in the truth of

God that surpass any of the fountains of this world. God help us to know we have got to study the Word of God.

And then there is another essential in this matter of going deeper with God and that is *compassion for the lost,* it is care for the unsaved. Oh, how few people there are that regularly in their life service for God care for the unsaved. You will work by the side of a man for years in business and never speak to him about Jesus Christ. Doctors will treat men and go into the homes of unsaved men for years and never say anything to them about the diseases of their souls. Lawyers will talk to men as their clients, but never speak to them about Jesus Christ. God help you to know today that if you are going to go deeper with God you will have to have a love, an abiding compassion, for the lost world.

I remember the case of a banker. I said, ''I want you to speak to your cashier about his soul.'' I plead with him. Finally he consented to do it. He said, ''I believe it will kill me to talk to him.'' He was a fine man but had never talked to anyone about Christ. That evening when the bank closed they locked the door and he went into the office of the cashier and said, ''I want to see you.'' They sat there together. This president of the bank said, ''We have been here eleven years together and I have never talked to you about your soul. We have talked about money and politics and everything else. But,'' he said, ''I am a

Christian, though I have never told you I wanted
you to be a Christian.'' That cashier put his
hand on the knee of the president of the bank and
said, ''For eleven years I have wondered why you
did not talk to me about being saved.'' He said,
''Do you believe my soul is more important than
my relationship to this bank or more important
than politics?'' The president of the bank said,
''Yes, I do.'' He said, ''Why have you not talked
to me about it?''

I buried some years ago a fine young man, a
popular young man who was not a Christian.
Everybody loved him. He was a fine business
young fellow. I noticed that great crowd that
filled the church. All of us were sad that he was
not a Christian. I noticed as the crowd came
around to look for the last time on the face of the
young man, that there was one business man who
was the proprietor and owner of the business
house in which this young man had worked who
came and stood at the foot of the coffin and cried.
Sometimes he was standing; sometimes he was on
his knees. Just before the family came I looked
and he was all in a heap. I thought he must be
related to him. No, he was not. Before the family came, he stopped the crowd and said, ''This
boy worked for me six years. I am a member of
this church, a deacon; but,'' he said, ''never in
the six years that I worked with this boy did I
speak to him about Christ. I promoted him and
paid him a larger salary, but I never talked to him

about his soul; and my heart is breaking that I
did not care and did not speak to him about his
soul.''

The saddest picture at the Judgment Bar of
God is that man who stands there with the blood
of some unsaved soul on his hands.

When I was pastor a doctor called me down one
morning to the hospital. He said, ''Here is a
woman I want you to see.'' I went into the room.
There was a woman with a little, poor, emaciated
child in her arms. It was starving to death, though
the mother had sustenance and milk for it. It
did not have the digestive organs with which to
assimilate strength. The woman was in the bed.
I talked to her and she said, ''I am a backslider.
I am away from God, my husband has left me. I
am dying.'' I prayed with her; she came back to
Christ. As I went out of the room happy, the
doctor said, ''There is another I want you to
see.'' I went with him into the ward. There lay
a big, strong man, a white man, though his face
was as black as that hat. He was a foreman of
a bridgebuilding company. The doctor said,
''That man was taken with a disease last night.
Five doctors have examined him and they do not
know what is wrong.'' There he was with all of
his faculties, but he was dying. I stood there, and
while I was talking to him the Spirit of God said,
''Speak to him about his soul.'' I had an engagement down town. That engagement pressed me. I
said, ''I will go.'' I passed out of that room with-

out speaking to that man. That night he died and
went into eternity unprepared to meet God. A
thousand times I have seen the black face of that
man. God told me to speak to him and I did not.
God help you to quit neglecting your duty to the
unsaved world.

Do you love souls? If you love souls you can
go deeper with God.

Then there is another essential in this matter
of going deeper with God and that is the *enduring
power of the Divine Spirit*. He says, "If ye being
evil know how to give good gifts unto your children, how much more shall your heavenly Father
give the Holy Spirit to them that ask him." He
said, "Ye shall receive power after that the Holy
Ghost is come upon you." And the Holy Spirit is
promised to the believer and given to every Christian who will pay the price. I wonder how many
of us know that power. I will tell you, my friends,
you cannot go deeper with God in this life without the power of God in your life. It makes all
the difference in the world when the power of God
comes on a man.

I am thinking about a man in my pastorate, one
of the truest men I ever knew. He was a clerk in
a grocery store. He lived out in the suburbs. He
had never been to college. He never had much of
this world's goods. But, oh, that man was such
a power! He had the power of God on him.

I will tell you, my friends, there is no substitute
for the power of God in Christian service. The

power of God on your life for service, for living
right, for producing power and joy in the world,
you have got to have that. We need to get out of
our little lives into the deeper waters in order
that we may win people to Christ. He came "that
they might have life, and that they might have it
more abundantly." He said that from within you
"shall flow rivers of *living* water." God help you
today to desire and hunger for a deeper life with
God. I wonder how many today have a thirst
for that deeper life. Oh, my soul hungers this
morning as the hart for the water brook, so does
my heart pant for thee, O God.

CHAPTER VI

OUR HEAVENLY RECORD

WHAT IT OUGHT TO BE

I find in the 87th Psalm and the 6th verse this scripture: "The Lord shall count, when he writeth up the people, that this man was born there. As well the singers as the players on instruments shall be there: all my springs are in thee."

"Springs"—the sources of my joy, my peace, my power are in Christ.

It is very clearly stated in the Word of God, especially in Revelation, that God has some books. There is a Lamb's Book of Life. It says that they whose names were not found in the Book were cast into fire and brimstone. In other places it speaks of the "books," indicating that there are a number of books. In other places it says in the Word that we are to give an account at the Judgment Bar of God, not only for our deeds and our words, but for our thoughts; the imaginations of our hearts shall be brought to judgment. And, in consistency with the revelation elsewhere in the Bible, this scripture says that God is writing up the people. "The Lord will count, when he writeth up the people, that this man was born there."

The very birthplace of the people will be recorded. In another place it is said that the hairs of our heads are numbered and that there is not a falling sparrow but what God takes cognizance of it. God is looking after the little things in our lives and He is writing up our lives. He is making an eternal record of our deeds and of our conduct. It is an impartial record. It is a record that is made by the facts of our lives. This to me is a very solemn thought, that the eye of God never sleeps and the interest of God in me never abates, never slacks, and that He is making a record of my life, my character, my words, my deeds, the thoughts of my heart. And yonder at His Judgment Bar in the eternal records that record will be found.

Some time ago I was in a great federal building, a postoffice building, just finished at very large expense by the Government. The postmaster, or the one in charge of the building, took me through it and showed me its apartments, its furniture, its offices. He said, "There is one place in this building to which I cannot take you; to which I cannot go myself." He said, "In the basement of this building is a door leading into a winding secret stairway that has unseen windows in it looking into every room in this building. There are," he said, "just two keys to that door. One is in Washington in the hands of the chief of the detective staff. The other is in the hands of the Government's detective in this district." He said, "Every man that comes into the employ of this building knows that there is a secret, winding stairway; but he doesn't know when a detective is in that stairway looking down through an unseen window upon him." He said, "This is the Government's method of detecting wrong." He said, "Everyone of us in this building works every hour as in view of the eye of the arm of the law." I said in my heart, "That is the way every child of God is living every day of his life, in the sight of that all-seeing and sleepless eye of God." He never misses an incident or an imagination; and He says that He is writing up the people.

Now, if that be true, and I take it that it is true, what a solemnizing effect it ought to have upon us, what a serious life we ought to live! How we ought to conduct ourselves as constantly under the purview of God and in view of this record that is to be made up yonder! What sort of a record are you making for God to write down? What is your life; what are your words; what are the emotions and the passions of your heart; what are your ambitions and your plans? Oh, if that be so, you and I ought to live constantly the right sort of life.

Now, there are some things that I should like for God to write down about me. I am not saying that he has done it or can do it; but as I look on life and see the standard that God has set in His Book and the high ideals set out in the life of Jesus Christ and in the teachings of the Divine

Spirit, there are certain things that I would like to have God write down in His record of my life.

SALVATION BY THE BLOOD

I should like for Him to say that I am saved—saved right—saved the right way. If in that record He is putting it down and it is eternal, I want Him to write that this man, Lee Scarborough, was born again—saved and saved right. And, my friends, you can deceive each other. We can deceive our best friends and go along through life living the life of a hypocrite; but when God's eye looks on He sees the facts and He is not going to let anybody by in mercy who is not saved right. I do not want to take any chances on salvation. Some people say you are saved by joining the church. Well, I do not believe it; but I want to join the church. Some say you can be saved by being baptized. I do not believe it, but I want to be baptized and baptized right. I want my baptism to match the New Testament. I do. And I will tell you, my friends, I am unable to see how anybody can be satisfied with a Divine Ordinance that is not absolutely in accord with the Word of God. Some say you can be saved by being baptized and taking the Lord's Supper. Well, I do not believe it but I want to take the Lord's Supper. Some people say that you can be saved by a good life, a consistent life. Well, I know that is not so; but I want to live a consistent life. Some people say that you have got to be charitable and liberal and kind and sweet and joyful. Well, I do not believe any of those things save a man; but I want to be liberal and charitable and kind and sunshiny in my life. Oh, my friends, we ought not to take any chances on this matter of being saved. Somebody says that you are saved by hope. Then I want to be filled with hope that I may get whatever there is in that great grace that constantly comes into the soul and brightens the life.

The Word of God says that you are saved by the grace, by the regenerating power of the Holy Spirit, by the imputed righteousness of Jesus Christ, by the blood of Christ that cleanses from all sin. Then if that be so I want to come in reach of that blood. I want the imputed righteousness. I want that regeneration of the Spirit. I want when God looks down into my record that He shall see there that I have been saved according to what God requires. I do not believe in salvation in anything outside of the blood and His imputed righteousness.

I joined the church before I was saved. I did not think I was saved, but that good deacon who examined me thought I was saved and persuaded me to join the church. I was baptized; I took the Lord's Supper; and for two years I lived a reasonably consistent life. But I knew I was not saved. And I remember that I said to my father, "I want the church to take my name off of the roll and do what they please with me. I am not saved." I was not satisfied; but I shall never

forget that day when I was walking the street,
thirty-six years ago, when I trusted my soul into
the hands of the Lord Jesus Christ and got out
from behind the sheltering power of church mem-
bership and came out into the open and trusted the
Lord Jesus Christ as my Savior. Since that time
I have been baptized. I was not baptized before,
for you cannot really baptize a sinner. Since that
time I have given of my money and my love and
I have tried to preach the Gospel and live this life
in the light of the Judgment Bar of God. The one
thing I am holding on to is not what I was, nor
did, nor preached, nor have given, but what Jesus
Christ did to my poor soul when I trusted Him on
the day of salvation.

OBEDIENCE

Now, there is another thing I want God to say
about me, if He is writing up my character and
my life. I want Him to say that I am an obedient
child. I want Him to write down yonder in that
record that my life is conforming to His will and
that I am trying to do what He wants me to do.
I am sorry that all of my record has not been
obedient. There is one period of three months in
which I felt the call of God to preach and I fought
it and rebelled against it; but, thank God, on the
16th day of April in 1896, in Old Farnum Hall at
Yale University, in my room, on my bed, with a
broken heart I yielded and I thank God that since
that time I have been trying to do His will. And

so thoroughly do I believe in that doctrine, I was in love with a beautiful, charming woman and I wrote her that I wanted her to be my wife. I said, "In my next letter I am going to ask you to be my partner for life. But in this letter I ask you another question. God may call me to be a missionary in Africa or China or somewhere else. I want you to accept me as your husband on the basis that it may be that it means for us to go to China or somewhere else." And in my heart I said, "I will not form any alliances here that will keep me from doing the will of God."

The obedient life is the happy life, the conquering life. If you are disobedient to God, you are unhappy. There is no salvation in it; but, thank God, there is joy and power in it.

PURITY OF LIFE

There is another thing that I want the Savior to write down about me and that is (Oh, that it were true of everyone of us!), I want Him to write it down that I am trying the utmost of my life to live a separate life unto Jesus Christ. I believe that the child of God ought to live a clean life. I do not want any moving-picture going, or gambling, any card parties, any dancing, in my record. I do not want any lying or grafting in my record. I do not want to meet God with having taken money from men and widows and orphans unjustly. The separate life is the life that God's child ought to live. I will tell you none of us can win with half of our lives in the world and the other half in the church. Such a life will win nobody to Christ. The most serious thing we have in this life is our testimony to Christ. I do not want any of my children yonder at the Judgment Bar of God to raise any question about my life. I know some good men, ordinarily counted good, that tonight are standing in the way of their children by their temper or by their punishment or their treatment of those children. I know a man tonight to whom I have preached several times. He is a traveling man. And I never see him and preach to him that he does not weep; and I never preach to him that I do not call him to the Lord Jesus Christ. Every time he has started I have talked to him and he loves me and I love him. And every time he comes close to God and I ask him to accept the Savior he says, ''My father is in my way.'' And that man's father is a deacon in a church. Oh, my friends, the importance of our example before our children! Some women in society and in the church life and some young people in their influence are leading other people away from God. Now, I will tell you, my friends, that right along there is a very serious matter. I want God to write it down that I am trying to live for Him.

I know a young lady tonight who, unless there is a change in the attitude of her father towards her, I am afraid will never give her heart and life to Jesus Christ. Oh, my friend, is there anything wrong in your family? Have your children any confidence in you? Does your partner have any confidence in your life? Is your social life such that your religious life is unimpaired? God is looking down on us with that all-seeing eye and He has made a record.

If there is a backslider here tonight, you have no right to be a backslider. Out of gratitude to God you ought to come back to Him. In view of that eternal record you have to meet after a while, you ought to come back to God.

FAITHFULNESS

There is another thing I want God to write down in His record about me. I am not saying that He can do it; but I want Him to do it—to write that I am faithful, faithful to *His Bible*—faithful to His Bible.

I believe the Bible from lid to lid. I take it all —Jonah and the whale and every other miracle in it. I do not have any trouble with the miraculous in God's Word. My boy when fourteen years of age came home one Sunday after church and we were in the room waiting for dinner. We had had the story of Jonah and the whale in the Sunday-school lesson that morning. He said, "Daddy, I do not believe that story." I said, "What's the trouble, my boy?" He said, "I cannot understand how God could take care of a man three days and nights in the stomach of a whale and the whale in the sea." I said, "My boy, that is not my trouble at all. My difficulty is to understand how God made Jonah and how He made the whale. Why," I said, "if God could make as intricate a piece of machinery as Jonah and as the whale He could put them in any sort of combination and take care of both of them." "Oh," he said, "you mean to put God in, that explains and settles it all."

Oh, my friends, yonder some day I am going to meet the author of this Book; and I thank God, He can say up to this time that I have never doubted one syllable of it.

I want to be faithful to *His church*. If some of you men were to treat your wives like you treat your church, you would have had a separation long ago—or a flogging one. Christ says we ought to be as true to our churches as we are to our wives. I have no patience with the husband who goes around criticizing his wife, or with the woman who goes around criticizing her husband. You may have criticism to make; but you dishonor yourself when you give utterance to it. I have no patience with the man who goes around criticizing his church. The churches do not save; but they have been the vessel through which the people have heard of salvation through the ages.

I want Him to put it down that I am faithful to *His ministry*. Now people today in a very light way criticize preachers; but I will tell you, my friend, if that light criticism of preachers was taken away, the churches and the preachers would

be more powerful than they are today. If you do
not like your pastor, pray for him. God help us
to be faithful to Christ's ministry. I am giving
my life to the training of preachers. I bless God
for His preachers. I had a love letter from one
of them today. Oh, my friends, how I thank God
for the love of the ministry! I want God to put
it down that I am faithful to the ministry of His
churches.

My friends, we do not have to be successful.
The test of our religion is not our success. What
did Moses do that was a success? And yet, when
the angel of God picked out a committee to send
back to the earth to see what Jesus Christ was
doing down here, Moses was made chairman of
the committee; and he tonight is the second most
powerful man in this world. The Apostle Paul is
first. I speak of mere men. And yet what did
Moses do that was very successful in his day?
Your acceptance with God is not measured by
your success but by your faithfulness to God, to
God's Word, to God's Christ.

I want Him to write it down that I am faithful
to the Gospel of Jesus Christ. I do not claim
to be much of a preacher. I do not know much
poetry. I do not know much science. I do not
know much philosophy. I do not preach much of
those things. But, thank God, I have a simple record of having preached the plain, simple Gospel of
Jesus Christ.

B. H. Carroll, the greatest man I ever knew, as

he was about to die, a few days before he died, expecting me, as he wanted me, to succeed him as president of the seminary, I was in his room one day and he pulled himself up by my chair with his hands and looked me in the face. There were times when he looked like he was forty feet high. And he looked into my face and said, "My boy, on this Hill orthodoxy, the old truth is making one of its last stands and I want to deliver to you a charge and I do it in the blood of Jesus Christ." He said, "You will be elected president of the seminary. I want you, if there ever comes heresy in your faculty, to take it to your faculty. If they won't hear you, take it to the trustees. If they wont hear you take it to the conventions that appointed them. If they won't hear you, take it to the common Baptists. They will hear you. And," he said, "I charge you in the name of Jesus Christ to keep it lashed to the old Gospel of Jesus Christ." As long as I have influence in that institution, by the grace of God I will stand by the old Book.

WINNER OF SOULS

There is another thing I want God to write down about me in that record yonder. I want Him to write down that I am a soul-winner—a winner of souls.

There was a time when I wanted to be a great preacher. How joyous I was when somebody would come and say, "Brother Scarborough, that was a great sermon you preached." And I did not have any more sense than to believe them. My ambition was puffed up and I wanted to be somebody. But I thank God that I found out that I could not be a great preacher. It took me three years to find out; my friends found it out earlier. A great doctor was in my study and he and I had been praying. I unbosomed to him my ambition to be a great preacher and I bless God for the hour with that doctor. He said, ''Lee, I used to have an ambition to be a great doctor and I found out that I could not and I had an ambition then to be a good man for Jesus Christ and a winner of souls.'' And there that day in my study I died to the ambition to be a great preacher and there was born in my soul a hunger to be a good disciple of Jesus Christ and a winner of souls.

In that great Seventy-five Million Campaign when I was carrying such tremendous responsibilities and when a few days before Victory Week it was raining all over the South, one night after the doctor had extracted every tooth in my head, I was on my bed almost at the point of death. I said to my wife, ''In a little while it will all be over.'' I looked back over the last twenty-five years of my life and I saw a troupe, thank God, a long line that the Father had let me lead to Jesus Christ in these years; and as I thought I was going out into the other world, the one joy that was supreme was that He had let me lead somebody to Jesus Christ.

I have heard Dr. Truett tell the story of an incident that happened in his church in Dallas. He said there was a very devoted old woman who lived out in a house of two rooms on a back street in the suburbs of the city. She had a very wicked son, just one child. She was a widow. This boy had lived the most of his time in a saloon for years and had broken his mother's heart. For five years he had refused to go with her to church. One evening the boy was in his room on his bed asleep. And it came into the mother's heart to walk softly in her stocking feet, into his room and kneel at the bedside and ask God to let her carry her boy to church with her that night. And kneeling there her tears and emotion and deep-stirred soul got the best of her and expressed themselves in sobs and it awakened the boy. He jumped up and said, "Mother, what's the matter?" And she said, "Oh, I beg your pardon. I did not mean to waken you. I came in here to pray that God would let me take you with me to preaching, to hear my pastor preach tonight." He said, "Mother, if you will never ask me again I will go tonight." She said, "I cannot promise you that. I am going to follow you, like a mother, down to the grave." He finally consented to go. He waited until late on purpose because he wanted the crowd to be there so that he could sit at the back. Finally they got there. There were just two seats left, right at the door. The mother let him go in first and she sat at the end. A great throng was there. I wish you could see that picture. There is the boy on the back seat with the mother between him and the door. That door leads to the street and that street leads to the saloon and that saloon leads to hell. Oh, how many men there are in this world, all between them and hell is the love of a mother! The preacher preached as only he can preach and after the sermon he gave the invitation. He said, "Is there one here tonight who wants to be saved?" God's power in answer to that mother's prayer took hold of that boy. Finally he started down the aisle and before he had gotten half way he had given his heart to Christ. After the crowd was dismissed the dear old mother got down on the floor in front of her boy and kissed his knees, kissed his eyes and kissed his hair; and then she got up and took the preacher by the feet and hugged his feet. Then she looked up into his face and said, "Pastor, it was through you tonight that my boy was saved." I have heard that preacher say, "I had rather have that testimony than to wear the crown of England."

God help us tonight to know that God is writing us up. We ought to be soul winners.

CHAPTER VII

THE LOVE THAT SERVES

I want to speak to you this morning on "The Love that Serves." And I read a good deal from the 21st chapter of John. It seems that John closed his book with the 20th chapter and then thought of another thing that he wanted to put in; and I am glad he did.

"After these things Jesus showed himself."

You will remember that at this time Jesus was raised from the dead and whatever He did He did in His resurrection body. And He is now, nearly two thousand years later, just the same as He was then and what He could do then in His resurrection body if it is His will He can do again. I do not understand all about the resurrection body. The scriptures have revealed to us very little about the resurrection body. In that wonderful chapter in Corinthians it has told us about its eternity, its immortality, its incorruptibleness and all of that, but just how Jesus looked and appeared, what change there was in His body, we do not know very much. We know that He could talk and walk. We know that He ate and the indication is that material substance was no barrier to Him, because He went in through closed doors with His resurrection body. But the joy to me is, my friends, that after His resurrection, He appeared and manifested Himself to His disciples.

"There were together Simon, Peter, and Thomas called Didymus, and Nathaniel of Cana in Galilee, and the sons of Zebedee, and two other of His disciples. Simon Peter saith unto them, I go a fishing. They say unto him, We also go with thee."

I think this action on the part of Simon and the disciples that followed him was an indication that they had been disappointed in the Kingdom Christ Jesus set up. They expected Him to build a great earthly Kingdom and that they would be the cabinet officers in that Kingdom. But Jesus came to found a spiritual Kingdom and Peter with his earthly ambition was disappointed when he found that Jesus had died and was to build a spiritual Kingdom. Oh, how slow in our carnal lives the gospel takes hold. What sorry Christians we have and church members, brother preachers, after we have preached to them one, two, three and four years and longer.

And Peter said to his brethren, "I am going back to the old job. I am disappointed. It is not as I thought it was going to be and I am going a-fishing." And they said, We are going with you." I think this is the first step in Peter's backsliding. My friends, it is a sad hour for any of us when we lose interest in the spirituality of Christ's Kingdom. It is the day when we begin to backslide and get away from God; and the sad part of it is, like Simon, we carry others with us. When I heard that man say here the other day that because of his backsliding he had carried his children and his wife away back with him I thought of my own case. I have been a backslider since I have been a Christian, but, thank God, since I have been a father and a husband that I have never led my family away from Jesus Christ. I wonder if any of you today remember someone you have led away off from God. God help you to go and bring them back.

"They went forth and entered into a ship immediately; and that night they caught nothing."

Just as you did when you got away from God. Oh, my friends, the saddest life is the life of withered leaves, the life of barren leaves. Of all the trees in the forest and all the trees whose leaves clapped and praised Jesus Christ in His earthly ministry, the saddest tree is that tree on which He pronounced His curse, that tree which was barren and brought forth no fruit. The barren life is the life that catches nothing for Jesus Christ.

"But when the morning was now come, Jesus stood on the shore": Thank God, He comes to His discouraged, defeated disciples. He saw them that night toiling all night and early in the morning He came; and listen at what He said:

"But the disciples knew not that it was Jesus."

They did not recognize Him. How often it is true that He comes to us in His providences and we do not recognize Him. Sometimes He comes in the dispoiling of our purposes, in adversity, in sickness, and sometimes He allows the crêpe to be hung on our doors. It is Christ visiting us with some spiritual blessing. I wonder if we have an eye to see him and a heart to love Him when He comes.

I went to a sad home one morning to officiate in the funeral of an only child who had died, a beautiful little curly-headed boy four or five years of age. Suddenly God took him. Both of the parents were church members—the father just a church member, the mother a devoted Christian. Before the crowd gathered that morning out of the family room the father and mother came to look for the last time upon the face of their little darling, dead child; and I stood by the open coffin with them. Tears, unrestrained, came gushing from the eyes of the broken-hearted mother. The father was tearless. He stood there with clenched fists and with a rebellious heart and with a stubborn will. There as he looked into the face of his child he turned his face towards God and I saw him with clenched fists shake his fists in the face of God. On the other hand, the mother with open palm turned her face toward God and prayed about like this:

A MOTHER'S PRAYER

"We thank thee, dear Father, that thou didst let this little flower bloom in the garden of our hearts. Life has been sweeter by his coming. And since it is thy will that he should be transplanted to the garden of God, we thank thee for the mercy that comes in his place and for the joy that comes amid our sorrow. 'The Lord gave, the Lord hath taken away; blessed be the name of the Lord.' Heaven will be more real and nearer and sweeter and life will be more solemn and there will be a deeper longing in our souls for righteousness and power from God because of the homegoing of the little baby."

Now, the difference between the father and the mother at that funeral was that the mother saw Jesus on the shore and recognized Him and the father did not recognize the coming Savior.

Oh, my friends, you and I need to learn to submit to all the good providences of God, remembering that "all things work together for good to them that love God."

"Then Jesus saith unto them, Children, have ye any meat? Have you caught anything? Have you anything to feed the inner man on?"

"They answered him, 'No.' And he said unto them, Cast the net on the right side of the ship, and ye shall find."

I wonder if there are here this morning those who have been fishing on the wrong side of the boat.

THE SIN OF DISOBEDIENCE

A group of young ladies in this community met the other evening for a prayer meeting. Practically everyone of them had been indulging in wrong pleasures. And they got together thinking about how they could win souls to Christ. They had not gotten far along in their prayers and in their consultation about it until they discovered they had to give up something; and there they gave up the dance and these worldly pleasures, and immediately they led one of their own number to Jesus Christ. They had been fishing and had caught nothing, but they had been fishing on the wrong side of the boat. I want to tell you you cannot dance and play cards and gamble and lie and do these things wrong in the sight of the Lord Jesus Christ and have power to win souls. The reason so many people are going down to hell today, the reason why it is so hard to revive a church, is because they have been fishing on the wrong side of the boat.

Jesus said:

"Cast the net on the right side of the ship, and ye shall find. They cast therefore and now they were not able to draw it for the multitude of fishes."

I tell you the obedient life is the happiest life, is the most powerful life; and it is the only soul-winning life.

"Therefore that disciple whom Jesus loved saith unto Peter, 'It is the Lord.' "

It was the eye of love that discovered the risen Savior.

"Now when Simon Peter heard that it was the Lord, he girt his fisher's coat unto him (for he was naked) and did cast himself into the sea."

LOVE AND FAITH

Here is a characteristic in John—the eye of love that sees the Savior,—and a characteristic in Peter —that bold, adventurous faith that overrides difficulties,—which I wish every child of God had.

"And the other disciples came in a little ship; (for they were not far from land, but as it were two hundred cubits), dragging the net with fishes. As soon as they were come to land, they saw a fire of coals there, and fish laid thereon, and bread."

I never read that scripture that I do not ask myself the question, "Who made that fire and fried those fish and made that bread?" Why, my friends, it was the loving, compassionate care of the Savior getting ready to warm and feed His disciples. I bless God that on the shore of every storm-tossed disciple there is a loving Savior that has a warm fire and delicate meal if you will come to the shore where He now is.

"Jesus saith unto them, 'Bring of the fish which ye have now caught.' "

Jesus wanted them to take the fish He had

caught and they had caught and put them together. He wants us to get the joy of His service
and in the joining of the two there shall be fellowship and power.

SUPREME LOVE

"So when they had dined, Jesus saith to Simon
Peter, Simon, son of Jonas, lovest thou me more
than these?"

You know what He meant by that question. It
was a question of comparison and contrast. I
think He meant a good deal more than we ordinarily say. I think He meant to say, "Simon, do
you love me more than you do these disciples of
mine, more than your companions of pleasure,
your companions of business?" I think He meant
more than that. "Do you love me more than you
do these fish and this fishing tackle, representing
your business and your pleasure? Do you love me
more than you do your business or your pleasure
or your companions?" I think the Lord here
meant to include Peter's wife, and children if he
had any, in his little home up yonder. I bring
that question to your hearts this morning.

"He saith unto him, Yea, Lord; thou knowest
that I love thee. He saith unto him, *Feed my
lambs.*"

And the second time He asked the question and
Peter confessed that he loved Him, He said, "*Feed
my sheep.*" The third time he asked and Peter
was grieved and he said:

"Lord, thou knowest all things; thou knowest
that I love thee. Jesus saith unto him, '*Feed my
sheep.*' "

Jesus Christ was getting ready to go home and
turn over to these disciples the salvation of this
world. Oh, what a bold act, to turn over to a few
men and women the task of bringing this world
home to God! But He did it. He was getting
ready to go back; but before He went He said,
"I have a question to ask you. It is a question
of how much you love me." I thank God for this
little incident here in the life of the Savior. It
showed that His heart hungered for love. Brother
pastor, I thank God that here Jesus Christ showed
that He craves the love of men. He was not satisfied with the love of the Father, the love of the
Spirit, the love and admiration and glory of the
eternal home; but He wanted the love of bold,
plain, common men of the market and of the mart.
And I am honored this morning to remember that
Jesus wants me to love Him. And He wants you
and me to tell Him that we love Him. There is a
good deal of sentiment in me, my friends; and
I want my children and my wife to tell me that they
love me. I do. My first child had the habit every
day I was at home of coming and climbing up into
my lap and saying, "Daddy, there's got to be some
loving done now." I like even yet, after having
been married twenty-one years, to have that little
woman who is the partner of my sorrows and my
joys, to say, "I love you." I like it. And I be-

lieve that Jesus Christ likes it. I believe He
wants us to tell Him how much we love Him.

THE RIGHT TO DEMAND BEST LOVE

Peter said:

"Lord, thou knowest all things; thou knowest
that I love thee."

I believe Jesus Christ had a right to ask Peter
this question; and He has a right to ask you and
me. He has saved us and kept us and given us
His life and His joy and His peace. I believe
He has a right to demand of us the best love of our
souls.

I had the pleasure of having my mother live
with me after I was married for many years. She
died at the age of eighty-one. A little while before she died—crippled, with a broken hand, paralyzed in her back and slow of walk and lonely, it
was my pleasure every morning to go by her room
next to ours and pick her up out of the arm chair
and let her lean on my strong arm and go with
her in to the table. One morning she said, "Son,
are you not tired of helping your old mother? It
looks like the Lord would take me home and get
me out of the way." I sat her at the table and
got down at her knee and said, "Mother, I wish
you would not think of it that way. There is no
greater joy to me than to help you and to make
you have the only joy you can have in your old
age. Why," I said, "you have a right to my

best love. You went to the edge of the grave that I might have life. It was your strength that sustained me in those early years. It was your prayer and love that sustained me when there was nobody else to care for me. And in answer to your prayers I have accomplished all that I have done for the Master." After that breakfast I went to my study and I said, "Yes, Mother has a right to my best love; and how much more my Savior has a right to my best love." And I bring His question to you this morning. I want to tell you the way you answer this question decides some things in your life.

IT DECIDES PRAYER

It decides our access in prayer. I believe Jesus Christ has established the homelife on somewhat the same basis as the heavenly home. The child that loves the father and mother most is the one that gets what it wants. I remember when our oldest child was five years of age. I said to my wife, "I am going into the study and lock the door. I must have some time with my Bible. Do not let anyone come while I am there." I went into the study and locked the door. In a little while I heard a little, tender hand knocking at the door. I have never been able to keep the door locked when that knock came. And I opened the door and the little boy came in and stood there between my knees and asked me for something. I said, "Son, you know Daddy doesn't want you to have that." Obedient child that he was, he went out and as he passed out the door he stood there and looked back, then closed it, and then opened it and looked in again through the opening and said, "Daddy, you know Warrenie loves Daddy best of all." I said, "All right, son you can have what you want." I will tell you, my friends, I believe if God's children can climb up on the Father's knees and say, "Thou knowest, dear Savior, that I love thee best of all," I believe a power of evangelism will come into this town that nothing else can bring.

IT DECIDES POWER

Then there is another thing it decides. It decides your power in the Holy Ghost. This happened just before Pentecost. Simon had a few days before been lying and crying; but here, just a few days after this, He is preaching with the mighty power of the Spirit of God on him. I want to tell you, my friends, how much you love Jesus Christ decides your power with God. It is not how much Greek or how much Hebrew you know, nor where you stand in society, nor where you stand in the business world. It is how much you love Jesus Christ that decides your power with God. God will give His power to the one that loves Him most.

I was helping in a meeting at Midland years ago —150 miles west of Abilene, where I was then pastor. The T. & P. train left Midland at six o'clock in the afternoon going to Abilene and reaching there about midnight. On the morning of the last

day of the meeting I had a call, an especially urg-
ent appeal, to come home that evening, leaving
Midland at six o'clock and missing the evening
service. I had been talking with the pastor about
it. About that time a letter was put into my hands
from my wife. She said, "Our boy is very sick.
The doctor has just left and he says he has pneumonia." She did not say come home. She never
has said it in 450 meetings I have held since I have
been married about twenty-one years, and if the
time were all put together I have been away from
my family sixteen years of the twenty-one. She
never has called me home. She did not say come
home, but I will tell you something else did say
come home. I gave the letter to the pastor. He
read it. I said to him, "If I go on the six o'clock
train I will miss the night service. If I wait and
do not go until tomorrow, it will be midnight tomorrow night before I can get home and my child
might be dead by that time." The pastor said,
"Do as you please. Do what the Lord tells you
to do. But," he said, "I want you to remember
that that big cowman and his wife and his daughter have come for seventy-five miles from their
ranch to hear you tonight and you have a hold on
them that nobody else has." And I went into
my room and prayed about the matter. There I
stood, on one side of me my sick boy and on the
other side stood the big cowman and his wife and
his daughter; and this question came to me, "Lovest thou me more than these?" And I had to de-

cide between soul-winning and going to my child. I thank God I answered it right. I said, "By the grace of God I will commit my child to Christ and I will stay here and win those people, if I can." My friends, that night was the greatest night I ever saw. I had not finished preaching when that cowman got up and said, "I cannot stand it. I have got to be saved." And his wife and daughter came into the altar with him and all of them with a dozen others were saved that night. And when I got home that next night my boy did not have pneumonia and was well.

Do you want to win somebody to Christ? Do you want to have a Pentecost in your church and in your life? God help us today to love Jesus Christ supremely in our souls and then go to work for Him. "If you love me, feed my lambs." The love that serves! God pity the man that loves and does nothing else.

I saw a man who neglected his family and his wife worked out in the field when he himself ought to have been at work. I asked him if he loved his family; and he said, "Of course, I love them." I said, "If you love them, it looks like you would do something for them."

God help us to go out and work for Christ because we love Him. This is the supreme passion and the supreme motive of service. I wonder how much you love Him today. How much do you love Him today? God help you to manifest your love for Christ by going to work for Him. There is nothing needed more in this town than the love that separates from sin and lives the consecrated life. If you will get the love of God in your church members, you will see dancing and card parties, and the devil knows what else, going out the back door and souls will be coming in.

CHAPTER VIII

GLORYING IN THE CROSS—THE PRECIOUS BLOOD

I want to talk to you this morning about this scripture:

"But God forbid that I should glory save in the cross of our Lord Jesus Christ, through whom the world hath been crucified unto me and I unto the world."

That is the 14th verse of the 6th chapter of Galatians. And I read from I Peter 1 :18, 19:

"Forasmuch as ye know that ye were not redeemed with corruptible things, as silver and gold, from your vain conversation received by tradition from your fathers; But with the precious blood of Christ, as of a lamb without blemish and without spot."

My subject this morning is glorying in the cross of Christ—the precious blood of Jesus. I want you to look in the first place at who it was that used this language. It was the Apostle Paul as he was inspired by the Divine Spirit. I think that he is God's top man in all history and he had had many things that he could boast of and glory in; but he said, "I glory in nothing save the cross of

the Lord Jesus Christ.'' He could have gloried in
his great intellectual powers, for no man has more
thoroughly influenced the world than the strong
intellectual power of the Apostle Paul. He could
have gloried in his great spiritual power, for no
man has written or spoken with more spiritual
power than the Apostle Paul. He could have gloried in the work he had done for the Savior, because he had builded churches and started missionary plans and ordained and called out preachers
and won more people to Christ than any man in
his day and probably more than any man in all
the days. He could have boasted of what he had
written, because he wrote more profoundly and
his writings have been read and honored more in
the world than the writings of any other man in
all the world. But Paul said, ''I turn away from
all these things and I glory only in the cross of
the Lord Jesus Christ.'' He did not say that he
gloried in the life of Jesus, nor in the power of
Jesus, nor in the wonderful goodness and holiness
of Jesus, nor in His miracles, nor in His teachings, nor in His wonderful personal power. He
did not say that he gloried in the Kingdom that
He came to set up or in His resurrection and
ascension or in His intercession at the right hand
of the Throne of God; but he picked out His death,
not His life, but His death, not His crown, but His
sufferings, not His glory. But he said, ''I glory
most in His cross, in His death, in His sufferings.''

THE MEANING OF THE CROSS

I wonder, my friends, why it was the Apostle Paul could say what he did. It is all found in the meaning of the message of Christ's cross. What does the cross of Christ mean to the Apostle Paul and to all the saved people and to this lost world? That is the great question and it is about that that I wish to speak this morning; and the first thing I wish to say about His cross is that it *expresses the depth of sin*. The cross of Jesus Christ tells that there is something wrong with the world. If the Holy One, if the best man that ever lived, if the Son of God was led yonder to that cruel death of dishonor, if the best man, even the Son of God must die on the cruel cross, there must be something dreadfully wrong with men. And there on the cross is described the iniquity of sin, the diabolism of sin, the awful meaning of sin.

I saw a beautiful young woman whose life had been ravished by a passionate negro and I saw the young woman there in all the shame that came from that awful crime. I said not in that crime is the description of the darkness of sin. I have seen sorrow come into the home. I saw the little child killed by the drunken father. I saw the wife beaten almost to death by the drunken husband. I have seen the awful wreck of sin; but not in any of these is the last and final description of the awfulness of sin. But I must go yonder to Calvary's Cross and inquire Who is dying. It is Jesus the

Son of God, the son of Mary, the purest and best and holiest and most powerful man of this earth, dying, not for His sins but for ours. And there in that cross of Christ God tells the awful story of how bad men are. Oh, my friend, today look at the Cross of Calvary and turn away from your sins.

I wish to say in the next place that the Cross of Christ *exemplifies the highest love even of God.* There is no finer expression in all the world of how much God loves you and me and the lost world than in the cross of Jesus Christ. "God so loved the world that He gave His Son," not His gold, and He owns all the gold of the mines in the world; not His oil, and all the oil in the bowels of the earth is God's oil; not the cattle on the thousand hills; not the lands; not the worlds; not the stars and the suns. It did not say that He so loved the world that He gave His shining planets; but He gave up His only begotten Son in order that He might show men how much He loved them. There is nowhere expressed in all the world a limit to God's affection for men.

I heard a story of a young man and a young woman, I think it was in Houston, Texas. The young man, a clerk, was standing on the curbstone one day when business was dull. He looked up the street and saw an excitement. It came nearer and nearer. He saw a horse to a buggy running away; and the buggy came down the street closer and closer. He saw a frantic woman holding the lines.

The people gave way, some of them trying in vain to head off the horse. But when they got a little closer this young man saw that the young woman holding those reins was the young woman whom only a few weeks before he had promised to take as his life companion; and without thinking of his own life he rushed out and caught hold of the bridle bits. The horse was so enraged that it picked him up and carried him from side to side. What was in his heart? He was trying to save one he loved. And finally he swung the head of the horse and in doing it the horse fell and fell on him. They took him out, bleeding at the mouth and at the ears and at the nose. The beautiful young woman kneeled down over him and he said with his dying words, "Mildred, I loved you, didn't I?"

I tell you, God from Calvary, sending His Son to die for you and me, looks down and says, "I loved you, didn't I?" It is the finest expression in all the world of how God loves the sinner.

Not only is that true, but I have this to say also about this cross of Jesus Christ. It is *God's only method of saving a lost world.* On the two arms of the cross God has hung the salvation of this world. The cross of Christ is God's ultimatum to a rebellious world; and if they do not accept Him there is no other remedy. I say it again while I am here among you I do not want anybody to mistake the gospel I preach. I am trying to swing all the gospel I preach and practice and live and teach around the cross of the Lord Jesus Christ.

Oh, my friend, it is God's only method of salvation —not by the waters of baptism, not by the bread and the wine of the communion, not by the commendable things of a moral life, not by liberality; but if men are saved at all they are saved by the application of the blood of the Lord Jesus Christ to their repenting, believing souls. It is God's only method to save a lost world. If I had a life to live I would bring it to the cross of Christ. If I had a family to rear I would rear them around the cross of Christ. If I had a church to build I would build it around the cross of Christ. If I had a seminary to build I would build it around the cross of Christ. Oh, my friend, if I had a world to save I would bring it to the cross of Jesus Christ. It is God's one and only method of saving a lost world.

I want to say also about this cross that *it is the only message of the ministry,* whether they teach or preach or testify or sing or whatever they do. The one message that God has given to this world is in the blood of the cross of the Lord Jesus Christ. It is that and that alone that they should preach. Somebody said that "all roads lead to Rome." Somebody said that "all the truth of God's Word leads to the cross of Christ." In the British Navy I am told that every rope has a scarlet thread in it and everywhere you cut one of those ropes you find in it that scarlet thread. I will tell you, my friend, all the truth that the preachers preach and the teachers teach ought to have the scarlet thread in it. How this old world needs the message of the cross of the Lord Jesus Christ! Paul said, "I am determined to know nothing among you save the cross of our Lord Jesus Christ;" and he said, "God forbid that I should glory save in the cross of the Lord Jesus Christ."

I want to say another thing about the cross of Christ and that is that *it is an insignia—a sign— of our universal and eternal triumph.* It is the sign of victory. I bless God that the blood of the cross of Jesus Christ can conquer any sin. It can conquer any seething iniquity that ever came into this old world. If you are a drunkard the blood of Jesus Christ can save you. If you are an adulterer the blood of Jesus Christ can save you. If you are a murderer, a thief, it matters not what you are, the blood of Jesus Christ can take all the stain out of the soul that trusts the Lord Jesus Christ.

In Rev. 7:13 ff. there is a description that John makes of a great company that he saw. He describes that company. He says an angel said, "These are they that came out of much tribulation and have washed their robes in the blood of the Lamb." And in Rev. 12:11 it is said that they overcame him, Satan, down in the world by the blood of the Lamb. It was the blood of the Lord that conquered down here and up yonder. I bless God that the insignia of our universal triumph over sin is the cross of the Lord Jesus

Christ. It is the sign of our victory. Have you had a temptation, a sin? Bring it to the cross of Christ. Have you a lost loved one? Bring him to the cross of Jesus Christ, knowing that the blood of Jesus can cleanse and save and forgive every sin. God help you to know today that there is your chance to win over sin.

I held a meeting in Southwest Texas, one of the greatest meetings I ever saw. In the first day of that meeting somebody got up and said, "I want you to pray for the worst man in South Texas." I think in the next five minutes a dozen people repeated that request and said that man was their burden. After the service I said, "Who is this man?" They told me about him. He owned, out yonder seven miles, a saloon. The town in which I was holding the meeting was a prohibition town. He was always getting into trouble. Only a few weeks before that he had beaten a man up with a six-shooter. In a day or two I met his wife, whom I remembered as a friend of mine in my first pastorate. I had tried to win her to Christ. She said, "I want you to come and take dinner with us." I said, "I will go next Sunday morning if you will get your husband to come and hear me preach Sunday morning." Next day she came and said, "He has promised to come with me." He had not been to church in nine years and hated preachers. Saturday night that man got on my heart. I scarcely slept a wink for praying for that man's salvation. Next morning when the crowd came

I saw this man and his wife, and his grown
daughter by his first wife, and a little baby come
in and sit down fifteen seats away. I called his
wife and said, "I am going to preach for your
husband; I do not want you to let the child bother
him. If the baby cries you take it out; do not let
him leave with it." And that morning I preached.
I shall never forget the service. God's mighty
power came. While I was preaching this woman
put her head on her husband's shoulder and was
saved. In a little while the grown daughter put
her head on the other shoulder of her father and
was saved. And there between those loved ones
he sat and wept. And when I made a proposition
to those who would seek Christ he came first and
sat there on the front seat. I do not exaggerate
it when I tell you that there were two hundred
people who sobbed or shouted instantly and out
loud as he came down the aisle. I said, "Is there
a man, not a woman, but a man who wants to
pray for this man here?" I am sure that two
hundred grown men made for that man instantly
and I led the prayer and I held the poor sinner ruined by sin up to Almighty God. When
the prayer was over I said, "If there is any one
who will trust Christ, come give me your hand."
Scores came. He was still sitting there. He mo-
tioned to me to come to him. And he looked at
me and said, "Preacher, for twenty-five years I
have been the meanest soul out of hell. I have a
question to ask you. Do you believe that the blood

of Jesus Christ can now cleanse me from all sin?''
I said, ''My friend, if you will trust the Lord Jesus
Christ He will save you.'' He trusted Him. I
said to him as he was joining the church, ''What
are you going to do with that saloon?'' He said,
''I have already closed it and shut it up.'' And
I understand he has lived for God since that day.
I say to you today that the cross of the Lord Jesus
Christ is the insignia of victory over the worst of
sins. I commend to you today the cross of the
Lord Jesus Christ.

And in concluding I ask a question:

WHAT ARE WE GOING TO DO WITH THE CROSS OF JESUS CHRIST?

What are we going to do with the cross of Jesus
Christ? It is here in the hands of the preachers,
in the hands of the Sunday-school teachers, in
the hands of all the saved, and on the hands of the
unsaved man. For me I am going to accept its
saving power. I am going to express in my life
my gratitude to Almighty God for the cross of
Jesus Christ. Oh, today, my soul is so grateful
for a consecrated mother, for a good father for a
splendid, consecrated, faithful, believing, unselfish
wife who for these twenty-one years has helped me
to bear my sorrows and carry my burdens. I am
grateful for six well and splendid children. I am
grateful that God called me to preach and has led
me to bring somebody to Christ. But I am most
grateful for the cross of the Lord Jesus Christ

that saved me and keeps me today. What are you going to do with that cross? I am not only going to accept it; I am going to preach it and try to bring a lost world to its efficacious power. Oh, today what are you going to do with the cross of Christ? Do you love it? Do you honor it? Do you glory in it? It is the only thing, Paul says, that we ought to glory in.

THE CROSS OF THE LORD JESUS CHRIST IS GOD'S CALL TO SERVICE

There is another thing I want you to hear and that is that the cross of the Lord Jesus Christ is God's call to service. Do you hear its call? I have heard the call that comes from the lips of mother and father. I have heard the call that comes from the prayer of the mother. I did not know it until after I had surrendered to preach that my little mother when I was three weeks of age crawled out of bed and on her knees walked across the room to my cradle and offered a prayer that God would call me to preach. Oh, how grateful I am for that! I have heard the call that comes from the dying man, the man punished in hell. I have heard the voice of Dives saying, "Go to my father's house. I have five brothers and they will repent." But, oh, my friends, the most pungent, the most powerful call I have ever heard to give my life to the service of God is the call of Christ's cross. You and I today have no right to live out of the service of God when we hear the call of

Christ's cross. Do you hear it? I wonder if I am speaking to some young man who has heard the call of God to preach, in your prayers, in the sermon you have heard, when you read the Bible, you have heard the whispering of the Divine Spirit—"Give me thy life: I want you to preach." I wonder if I am not speaking to some young woman who has heard the call of God to be a missionary—the call of the foreign field. I wonder this morning if I am not speaking to some young woman who has heard the call of God to be a trained nurse. I wonder if I am not speaking to some young woman or some young man who has a voice that God needs in His service. I bless God for men that are not called to preach who have a talent to sing which they are willing to give to Christ. Will you give that voice to Him today?

I would make you hear this morning if I could the call of the cross of the Lord Jesus Christ. Oh, hear and answer that call. I thank God for twenty-five years now I have answered that call to preach and I have never seen a moment when I regretted that I answered it.

Is there a man or a woman in this audience that has made money? Do you hear the call of God to use that money for the glory of Jesus Christ? Oh, my friend, you have no right to selfishly use all the money that God enables you to make here out of oil and other things. Oh, that you would hear the call of God to use that money for the glory of Christ.

Everyone of us is by the cross of Christ called to the service of God. God help us today to hear that call and answer that call and cling to the cross of Christ as the source of all our hopes and of all our powers and of all of our glorying in this life and the life to come.